The Wor Company of Fletchers of London: The Early Centuries, c.1371–c.1571

Hannes Kleineke

THE WORSHIPFUL COMPANY OF FLETCHERS
2021

ISBN 978-1-3999-0166-6

Printed by 4word Ltd, Bath

Contents

FIG. 1: From left to right: Duncan Garland, Master 2019–20; Stuart Robbens, Master 2020–21; Anne Curry, Master 2021–22; Philip Shears, Upper Warden 2021–22; Andrew Trapnell, Renter Warden 2021–22.

Foreword

In celebrating its 650th anniversary, the Worshipful Company of Fletchers is delighted to publish a new history of its first centuries, all the more so as it has been researched and written by one of our own liverymen, Dr. Hannes Kleineke. As Masters in the anniversary year, we extend our grateful thanks to Hannes on behalf of the Company.

We thank you for purchasing the book, since all income will go to The Fletchers Trust, our charity, whose main focus is the support of all levels of the disabled archery community, including Team GB Paralympic Archers.

At one time the Fletchers and Bowyers may well have been one Company but by 7 March 1371 the Fletchers had petitioned the Lord Mayor and Aldermen for the two trades to be separate. They have remained so ever since, with the Fletchers Company considered to be a Company established by prescription. It seems very appropriate that on 22 July 2020 the Company petitioned The Queen's Most Excellent Majesty in Council for the grant of a Royal Charter and that this Grant was approved by the Privy Council in this, our 650th anniversary year.

It is our sincere wish that our ancient and honourable Company continues to flourish, root and branch, for many years to come.

Stuart Robbens, Master 2020–21
Anne Curry, Master 2021–22

List of Illustrations

FRONT COVER: Medieval Fletchers at Work, from a fourteenth-century MS Romance of Alexander. Bodleian Library, MS Bodley 264, f. 123v (detail). Photo Bodleian Libraries.

FIG. 1: Master, Past Masters and Wardens of the Worshipful Company of Fletchers, July 2021. © Worshipful Company of Fletchers. Photograph: John Leatherdale.

FIG. 2: Grant of arms to the Fletchers' Company of London by William Hawkeslowe, Clarenceux King of Arms, Guildhall Library, London, MS 21116. © Worshipful Company of Fletchers. Photograph: John Leatherdale.

FIG. 3: Quarterage roll of the Fletchers' Company, 1545–6. Among the members named are the widows Marion Romynge and Margaret Cony. Guildhall Library, London, MS 5977/1, m. 12. © Worshipful Company of Fletchers. Photograph: John Leatherdale.

FIG. 4: Panoramic View of London from the South Bank (detail), c.1616, by C.J. Vissher, showing the prominent spire of the Austin Friars (then the Dutch Church). © London Metropolitan Archives (City of London).

FIG. 5: Detail from the 'Agas' map of London c.1561, showing the area around St. Mary Axe, with the Fletchers' Hall at the upper (north-eastern) end of the street. © London Metropolitan Archives (City of London).

BACK COVER: Arms of the Worshipful Company of Fletchers, 2021.

List of Abbreviations

c.	circa
CCR	*Calendar of the Close Rolls*
CPR	*Calendar of the Patent Rolls*
d	dorse
d.	died
f(f).	folio(s)
fl.	*floruit* (was alive)
GL	Guildhall Library, London
LMA	London Metropolitan Archives
LP Hen. VIII	*Letters and Papers Foreign and Domestic of the Reign of Henry VIII*
mm.	membrane(s)
MS(S)	manuscript(s)
n.s.	new series
p(p).	page(s)
r	recto
rot(s).	rotulet(s)
TNA	The National Archives, Kew
v	verso
vol(s).	volume(s)

Preface

This short history of the London Fletchers Company during the first two centuries of its independent existence was prepared as part of the celebrations to mark the 650th anniversary of its separation from the Bowyers in or by 1371. It traces the history of the Company and its life from its heyday during the Hundred Years' War of the fourteenth and fifteenth centuries, when arrows in their thousands were needed to equip English armies fighting in France, through the religious upheavals of the mid sixteenth century, to the beginnings of its gradual decline in the reign of Elizabeth I, as archery increasingly became little more than a leisure pursuit. In an appendix, it provides the original texts and translations of the Company's early ordinances presented and enrolled at Guildhall up to the reign of Henry VII.

In the course of this project I have incurred a number of debts. I am grateful to the two successive Master Fletchers whose years of office straddle the anniversary year, Mr. Stuart Robbens and Professor Anne Curry, for their support, and for providing a foreword to the text. It goes without saying that the successful completion of the project owes much to the work and support of the Company's clerk, Miss Kate Pink. Anne Curry and Kate Pink, as well as Dr. Anne F. Sutton, Past Master John Dumbrell and Liveryman John Leatherdale, read drafts of the text, and provided many helpful comments. Caroline Barron, Justin Colson, Leslie Head, and Caroline Metcalfe all provided useful references and information. While the project was well under way before the onset of the Covid19 pandemic of 2020–21, the closure of most academic libraries and archives made research challenging. I am grateful to the staff of the National Archives and the London Metropolitan Archives, particularly Dr. Elizabeth Scudder of LMA, for their efforts in facilitating access to manuscript material at the times when this was briefly possible.

London, the feast of the Decollation of St. John the Baptist 2021.
H.K.

The Early Organisation of the Craft

The chronology of the evolution of London's livery companies from informal trade or craft associations, often with a religious element, to fully fledged corporate bodies owning property and governed by particular sets of ordinances has been extensively studied.[1] Within this wider frame-work individual companies underwent developments particular to them, and in the case of the crafts (as opposed to the mercantile companies) technological evolution was self-evidently an important factor in determining their fortunes. One field of technology that underwent repeated, and ultimately revolutionary, change in the later medieval period was that connected with warfare. As assault weapons evolved, so did the means of protection available to the combatant, but it was the long-distance weaponry that underwent the most dramatic developments. The crossbow was superseded by the long-bow, only for bows and arrows of all kinds to be displaced for their part by the new fire arms.[2] It was thus that the craft guilds that produced bows, bolts, arrows, and their constituent parts, such as bowstrings or arrow heads, enjoyed only a brief heyday in the mass manufacture of their products during

---

1   An accessible general summary is found in C.M. Barron, *London in the Later Middle Ages* (Oxford, 2004), pp. 199–234, and also see the literature cited there, particularly the classic discussion by G. Unwin, *The Gilds and Companies of London* (London, 1908). For the early period, see also D. Keene, 'English Urban Guilds, c.900–1300', in *Guilds and Association in Europe, 900–1900*, ed. I.A. Gadd and P. Wallis (2006), pp. 3–26; A.F. Sutton, 'The Silent Years of London Guild History before 1300: The Case of the Mercers', *Historical Research*, lxxi (1998), 121–41 and E. Veale, 'The "Great Twelve": Mistery and Fraternity in Thirteenth-Century London', *Historical Research*, lxiv (1991), 237–63.
2   There is an extensive literature on the development of gunpowder weaponry which lies outside the scope of the present study. A starting point for the debate over the connected theory of the 'medieval military revolution' is the compact summary given by K. DeVries, 'The Use of Gunpowder Weapons in the Wars of the Roses', in *Traditions and Transformations in Late Medieval England*, ed. D. Biggs, S.D. Michalove and A.C. Reeves (Leiden, 2002), pp. 21–38, at pp. 22–3, and also see more recently D. Spencer, *Royal and Urban Gunpowder Weapons in Late Medieval England* (Woodbridge, 2019).

the period of near-continuous warfare (mainly in France, but periodically also in Scotland or at home) from the mid fourteenth to the mid sixteenth century, before the evolution of gun-powder weaponry turned the practice of archery into a form of recreation that harked back to an earlier age, but was of increasingly limited consequence in real armed conflict.[3]

By the second half of the fourteenth century, years of campaigning on the continent combined with a fear of French raids on the English coast, had created a sustained high level of demand for arrows and crossbow bolts (or quarrels), beyond what was required anyway for hunting, self-defence, and from the 1360s officially-prescribed archery practice. This commercial factor may have played a central part in fostering the sense of importance that by early 1371 gave the Fletchers of the City of London the self-confidence to break free from their fellows who manufactured bows, and to seek the status of a company in their own right.[4]

The crafts that made the individual components of bows and arrows were highly specialised. The bowyers relied for the manufacture of their wares on the products of the longbowstringmakers (or stringers),[5] while the fletchers, whose concern were the shafts and flights of arrows, relied on a group of metalworkers, the arrowsmiths or arrowheadmakers, for the metal tips of their wares.[6] Bowyers and fletchers themselves were woodworkers, who prepared the wooden parts of bows and arrows and fitted them with the components purchased from these other craftsmen. The connexion between bows and arrows was an intimate one – the one being essentially useless without the other – and by the mid fourteenth century some London workshops combined the manufacture of the two finished articles under one roof. In their majority, however, the two crafts seem to have operated separately, and, whether or not an otherwise undocumented dispute went before, it seems to have been by mutual agreement that by the spring of 1371 the bowyers and fletchers had decided to go their separate ways, and to concentrate on the regulation of

---

3   On the early history of the London bowyers, see above all B. Megson, 'The Bowyers of London 1300–1550', *The London Journal*, xviii (1993), 1–13.

4   The provision of weaponry on a substantial scale was itself a development of the Hundred Years' War. Under earlier monarchs, individual archers had been left to their own devices in procuring armaments for the campaign on which they served: M. Prestwich, *War, Politics and Finance under Edward I* (London, 1972), pp. 105–6.

5   The Longbowstringmakers formed a company of their own in 1416. For that company's history down to its demise in the 1850s, see J.E. Oxley, *The Fletchers and Longbowstringmakers of London* (London, 1968), pp. 117–52.

6   There is a growing literature on medieval arrowheads. For a starting point see e.g. O. Jessop, 'A New Artefact Typology for the Study of Medieval Arrowheads', *Medieval Archaeology*, xl (1996), 192–205, and the older remarks on the typology of arrowheads by J.B. Ward-Perkins in the *London Museum Medieval Catalogue* (London, 1940), pp. 65–73; D. Starley, 'What's the Point? A Metallurgical Insight into Medieval Arrowheads', in *De Re Metallica: Uses of Metal in the Middle Ages*, ed. R. Bork with S. Montgomery, C. Neuman de Vegvar, E. Shortell and S. Walton (Aldershot, 2005), pp. 207–21.

their respective crafts.

If there was a catalyst for this development, if may have been the Crown's sudden repeated demands from the second half of 1369 for sheaves of arrows in their thousands, demand which had not been seen on this scale since the treaty of Brétigny of October 1360. Under the terms of this agreement King Edward III of England had agreed to give up his claim to the French crown in return for vast territorial concessions in France, while the French also agreed to pay a huge ransom for their King, John II, who had been taken prisoner by the English at the battle of Poitiers in September 1356. While the treaty led to a cessation of immediate hostilities, it did not provide for a lasting peace and in the spring of 1369 the new French King Charles V (John II's son) resumed the war.

In October 1369 the sheriffs of London were instructed to supply 1,000 sheaves of arrows to the Tower, and in February 1371 they were ordered to find a further 2,000 sheaves. In the autumn of 1369 the sheriffs in the rest of England were commanded in the same form to provide some 20,000 sheaves, while in February 1371 they were charged with finding a further 15,000. Such demands placed intolerable pressure on the makers of arrows everywhere. In 1369, more than one sheriff found himself unable to procure his full quota of arrows, and London's craftsmen seem to have absorbed some of the pressure. The King's officials made good part of the deficit by sourcing the required arrows themselves, presumably mostly in the capital, and charging the cost to the defaulting sheriffs' accounts. The Crown's reaffirmation of an existing ban on the export of weapons and armour did little to ease the pressure on the manufacturers, and it seems clear that in the haste to meet market demand corners were cut in some quarters, and some shoddy workmanship crept in. Good quality arrows required seasoned wood, and the emphasis of the King's instructions that the arrows delivered to the Tower should not be made of green wood suggests that the proper material was not always used, or perhaps even available in sufficient quantities. For many artisans there were quite literally not enough hours in the day, and the practice of working after dark and in poor light, banned by the Bowyers in March 1371, shortly after the separation of the two crafts, clearly also applied to the Fletchers who outlawed it a few years later, in 1432, along with the use of green wood. What seems clear is that the leading men of the crafts must have concluded that closer oversight was required, and there can be no doubt that London's civic authorities would have concurred.[7]

The exact date of the formal separation of Bowyers and Fletchers is not recorded, but it probably occurred in late 1370 or early 1371, for on 7 March 1371 leading representatives of the two crafts appeared at Guildhall and sought the sanction of the mayor and aldermen on four individuals who

---

7   *CCR*, 1369–74, pp. 41, 57–8, 114, 208–9; LMA, Letter Book K, f. 106v, see appendix below, no. 4.

disagreed with the decision. The four men in question, John Patyn, Robert atte Verne, Richard Prodhomme, and John Lyon, evidently had much to lose: as they expounded before the authorities at Guildhall, not only did they each have stocks of both bows and arrows that remained unsold, as well as part finished items (and thus presumably also stocks of raw materials), but some of them were training apprentices in each of the two crafts. In the first instance, the four men were given leave until the coming feast of Easter, which was then four weeks away, to choose one of the two trades, and to settle their outstanding affairs. Three of them apparently did so, but on 11 August the Bowyers again complained of atte Verne, who had continued to work as both and bowyer and fletcher. Atte Verne now chose the bowyer's craft, and on his submission to the mayor's authority was pardoned the fine that he should have incurred.[8] An even shiftier character was Patyn, who actively sought to circumvent the new regulations by setting one of his servants to work making and selling bows in Southwark, just outside the jurisdiction of the London authorities, while he himself ostensibly lived the life of a respectable fletcher within the City. In January 1375 he was fined 40s., but he had in any event died by the spring of 1376.[9]

While these were extreme examples of individuals whose activities were deemed so detrimental to good order as to require the official sanction of the mayor and aldermen, it is clear that ties between Fletchers and Bowyers remained close. On ceremonial occasions the men of the two companies often walked side by side, and for some events, such as the funeral in 1422 of the recently deceased Henry V, the two companies were even treated as one by the civic authorities.[10] There was finally some recognition of the insoluble connexion of the two trades in January 1429, when the ordinance of 1371 was amended to the effect that while Fletchers and Bowyers should not meddle in the manufacture of the other craft's products, or sell such goods by retail, they might nevertheless trade in them wholesale. By contrast, it was formally laid down at the same time that the raw materials required for the making of arrows, such as feathers and the wood for arrow shafts, would be subject to the inspection and survey of the Fletchers only, while the Bowyers should confine themselves to controlling the manufacture of bows and 'arquebusses'.[11]

If the disentanglement of their affairs thus occupied the Fletchers and Bowyers for some time, the leading members of the Fletchers' craft soon also set about regulating their own membership, and in 1403 presented a first set of ordinances before the mayor and aldermen. Under their terms,

---

8   *Memorials of London and London Life in the 13th, 14th and 15th Centuries* ed. H.T. Riley (London, 1868), pp. 348–50; LMA, Letter Book G, f. 266v. See appendix below, no. 1.

9   *Calendar of Plea and Memoranda Rolls of the City of London, 1364–81*, ed. A.H. Thomas (London, 1929), pp. 187–8.

10   LMA, Letter Book K, f. 1v.

11   LMA, Letter Book K, f. 63v.

the governance of the Company was vested in two wardens, to be elected annually on the feast of St. Edward, that is, the Translation of St. Edward the Confessor on 13 October.[12] This remained the normal start date for the Fletchers' year until 1542, but from 1544 to 1559 the annual changeover of the wardens took place on the feast of St. Clement (23 November). In 1560, the elections were moved to the Conversion of St. Paul (25 January),[13] and there they were to remain, although in 1566 – uniquely, as far as we can tell – the wardens' elections were held on St. George's day (23 April), but had reverted to 25 January by 1568.

Although annual elections of wardens were prescribed by the Company's early ordinances and seem to have been the Fletchers' normal practice for much of their history, re-election for a second term was possible, and may indeed have been common. It may be significant that the Company's fullest set of ordinances, those of 1484, did not restate the wardens' annual terms, since in the next few years successive pairs of wardens are known to have served in consecutive years: Robert Holmenby and Richard Baxster from 1488 to 1490, and Simon Motte and John Burdon from 1490 to 1492.[14] Indeed, as the Company's early quarterage rolls show, for a period of time in the 1520s the Fletchers' wardens were expressly elected to serve for two-year terms, but by the mid 1530s, the elections had once again returned to the annual cycle.[15]

The Company's early wardens were, as far as it is possible to tell, of equal status. This would change: by the 1560s it was normal practice to elect an experienced man who had served as warden on a previous occasion alongside a newcomer, and it is likely that this convention was established rather earlier. Without doubt there had always been distinctions between masters running their own shops, servants or journeymen, and apprentices, but it is only in the mid sixteenth century that a hierarchy among the senior members of the Company is clearly apparent. From the 1560s, the Fletchers' quarterage rolls began to separate out a body of former wardens, who were accorded the style of 'Master', a distinction which may already have been recognised by 1543, when the former warden John Wilshire invited to his funeral wake not only the current wardens but also 'such others as have been wardens'.[16] There can be little doubt that it was this group of 'Masters' that eventually morphed into the 'assistants' of the court, a term in formal use by 1572.[17]

In the final years of the sixteenth century, a further distinction also began

12   *Memorials of London* ed. Riley, p. 556; LMA, Letter Book I, f. 63v. See appendix below, no. 2.
13   The serving wardens, originally elected in November 1559, were re-elected in January 1560.
14   LMA, Journal 9, ff. 273, 280, 288v, 293.
15   GL, MS 5977/1, mm. 2–6.
16   GL, MSS 5977/2; 9171/11, f. 95v. For a more detailed discussion of the surviving quarterage rolls, see Oxley, *Fletchers and Longbowstringmakers*, pp. 18–20.
17   LMA, Repertory 17, f. 284v. Cf. appendix 2, no. 7, below.

to find reflection in the Company's quarterage rolls, which periodically noted the admission of an individual to the 'lyverey'. This was a manifestation in the official record of a practice by then established for more than a century. Distinctive liveries, even if consisting initially only of a common hood, had been worn by the members of at least some companies even by the later fourteenth century, when the practice formed part of a set of questions put to the London guilds by the Crown. Since many companies required their members to purchase their own livery gowns, which in some cases were renewed annually, the livery soon became restricted to the more substantial members who could afford this expense.[18] An inquiry held by the mayor and aldermen in 1501–2 found that there were fifty crafts in the City that had a livery. The greatest of them, the Grocers, Merchant Taylors and Drapers could boast eighty or more liverymen in their ranks, but in a majority of companies the livery numbered at most two dozen men or fewer, and at the lower end of the list the Fellmongers had just two men entitled to the livery. The Fletchers were at the time said to have eleven liverymen, comparable to the Bladesmiths and Wiresellers (who each had twelve), the Masons (who had eleven), and the Bowyers and Poulterers (who had ten each).[19] In 1484 the Fletchers' ordinances codified what was probably already the Company's established practice: those members approved to be 'of the Liuery or Clothing' were to buy once every three years before Easter their livery according to a common pattern chosen by the wardens with the assistance of two other 'honest men' of the Company. Anyone refusing to either wear or buy the livery was to be fined the substantial sum of 13s. 4d., half payable to the Company and half to the City. The social separation of the liverymen also found its reflection in wider Company life; in 1537 the will of the fletcher Hugh Partriche required that his post-funeral gathering was to be attended specifically by 'those of the clothing'.[20] At the same date, a list drawn up in the context of the military obligations of the citizens of London gives us an indication of the composition and subdivisions of the Company. The list which included masters, that is, former wardens, liverymen, and freemen householders, named ten masters, eight liverymen, and 26 freemen. By contrast, the corresponding Fletchers' quarterage roll for 1537–8 offers a further 22 names. Of these, one was a woman, and four others were probably either dead or infirm, as they subsequently disappear from the quarterage rolls.[21]

---

18 Barron, *London in the Later Middle Ages*, pp. 214–16.
19 LMA, Journal 10, f. 373v.
20 LMA, Letter Book L, f. 193v; GL, MS 9171/10, f. 299v.
21 For the woman, Margaret Cony, see below. The men who probably died before the military list was drawn up, were Henry Southworth, Geoffrey Meredith, Richard Aleyn and William Lamyston. The lists evidently had their origins in an initiative by Lord Mayor Sir Richard Gresham in the summer of 1538. In the aftermath of a series of popular uprisings in 1536–7 thought was given to the defence of London (and other towns), and the mayor reported to the King's minister Thomas Cromwell that the citizens were poorly provided with harness.

The remaining seventeen fletchers presumably fell into the lowest echelons of the Company, a group of whose status the Company's earliest surviving quarterage list (of 1519) affords us a unique glimpse. In that year, the final two men listed (Nicholas Bageley and Henry Fyssher) were explicitly styled 'yeomen'.[22] The usage of the term at that time was – much as it had been in the later medieval period – a fluid one, being applied in some instances to journeymen, in others to less prosperous householders, but the positioning of Bageley and Fyssher in the list leaves no doubt that they belonged to the lowest-ranking group among the Fletchers. What proportion of the Company such lowly members made up is perhaps indicated by the documentation of 1537, when the men omitted from the military list apparently accounted for about a quarter of the total membership.[23]

He thus proposed that the senior members of the London companies should be obliged to maintain certain armaments according to their economic standing, i.e. each aldermen twenty harnesses and halberds; each sheriff, ten; each warden of a company, four; each liveryman, two; and each householder outside the livery, one. This provision was to be inspected by the companies' wardens on a annual basis, and any defaulters were to be subject to a fine of 40s. *LP Hen. VIII*, xiii (2). 72; TNA, E 36/93, ff. 20v–21.

22   GL, MS 5977/1, m. 1d.
23   For the 'yeomanry' of the livery companies in the sixteenth century, see S. Rappaport, *Worlds within Worlds: Structures of Life in Sixteenth-Century London* (Cambridge, 1989), pp. 219–22. For the earlier period, Barron, *London in the Later Middle Ages*, pp. 211–14.

The Regulation of
the Craft

It is interesting to see that following their separation from the Bowyers, the Fletchers' process of regulating their craft was apparently haphazard, with regulations laid down piecemeal. There can be little doubt that from an early date the Fletchers' wardens exercised a degree of oversight both over the working practices and materials of the craft and the interaction of its members (such as the relationships of masters, journeymen and apprentices). Formal regulations, by contrast, were perhaps only brought to Guildhall to be put on the official record when the greater authority of the mayor and aldermen was deemed necessary for their enforcement. This might have been the case where individuals who fell outside, or refused to accept, the jurisdiction of the Fletchers' wardens, were concerned. These might include foreign or alien craftsmen, or, indeed, the inhabitants of Southwark where, as the case of John Patyn's servant shows, the powers of even the City remained limited. However, they could also include members of the Company itself, such as the four malcontents of 1371. Against this background, it becomes clear why the Fletchers' first concern should have been to lay down how their wardens should be chosen, leaving all else to these officials, once properly constituted under a procedure enrolled at Guildhall.

During the fifteenth century, the ordinances governing the various crafts and trades proliferated, not merely in London, but also elsewhere, and in parallel, increasing numbers of craft associations procured royal affirmations of their rights and powers. In 1437, the Crown agreed to a request by the Commons in Parliament that all companies and guilds that had acquired royal privileges should present these to the justices of the peace in their counties, or the civic and municipal authorities of their cities and towns. In London, where there was shortly after to be a challenge to the authority of the ruling elite that had not been seen since the 1370s, the mayor and aldermen set with aplomb about subduing some companies perceived to have become too big for their boots: even in 1438 the Brewers and Cordwainers were respectively required to renounce those of their

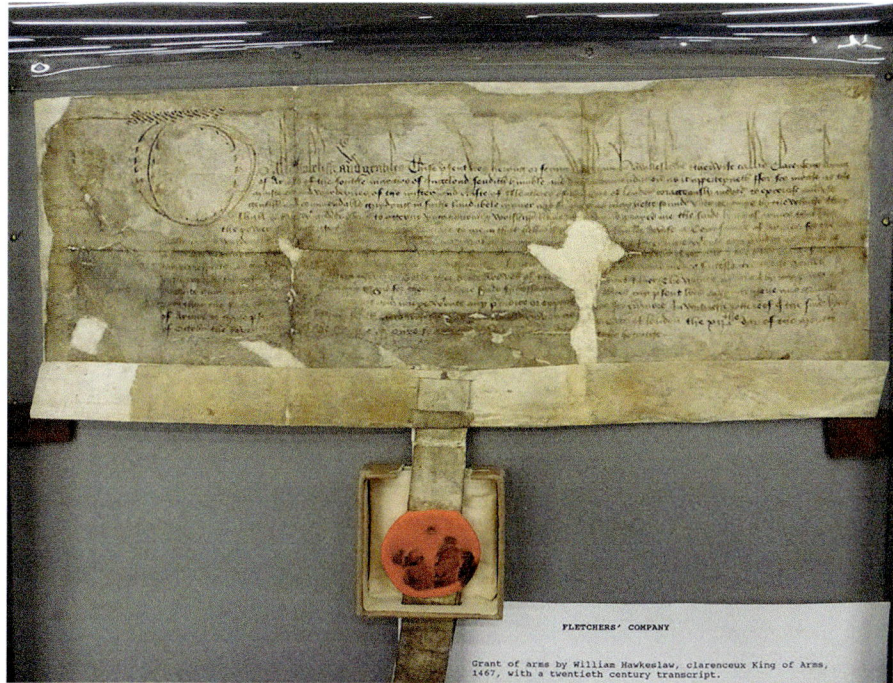

FIG. 2: Grant of arms to the Fletchers' Company of London by William Hawkeslowe,
Clarenceux King of Arms, Guildhall Library, London, MS 21116. © Worshipful Company
of Fletchers. Photograph: John Leatherdale.

privileges acquired by royal grant that were deemed prejudicial to the
interests of the City.[24]

As the Fletchers did not have a royal charter and instead relied on the
approval of the civic authorities for their ordinances and regulations, they fell
outside the purview of the statute of 1437. Their need to have any rules they
wished to see codified (as other companies did with their own ordinances)
approved at Guildhall, does, however, make the process particularly visible
to the modern observer.[25] Moreover, it is possible that as a Company that
had split from another, when other guilds were merging, the Fletchers had
a sense of 'needing to do things properly'. There is certainly such a sense in
their acquisition of a formal grant of arms from Clarenceux King of Arms

24   *Parliament Rolls of Medieval England, 1295–1504* ed. C. Given-Wilson *et al.* (16 vols., Woodbridge,
      2005), xi. 225–6; C.M. Barron, 'Ralph Holland and the London Radicals, 1438–1444', in
      The Medieval Town in England, 1200–1540, ed. R. Holt and G. Rosser (London, 1990), pp.
      160–83.
25   M.P. Davies, 'Crown, City and Guild in Late Medieval London', in *London and Beyond. Essays
      in Honour of Derek Keene*, ed. M.P. Davies and J.P. Galloway (London, 2012), pp. 247–68.

at the comparatively early date of 1467, and of an authorised crest twenty years later. Such heraldic bearings were routinely used by the companies in civic pageantry, but the practice of having these officially authorised by the royal heralds was still relatively new: only twelve other companies are known to have secured armorial patents at an earlier date.[26]

It took a further 20 years after the enrolment of the ordinance of 1403 for further Fletchers' rules to be placed on the record. In 1423, a prohibition of 'Sunday opening' was imposed, forbidding the fletchers to trade both on Sundays and on major feast days. It was, by contrast, not until the summer of 1432 that the old issue of poor workmanship and the use of inferior materials finally became the subject of an ordinance. It was now formally laid down that no enfranchised fletcher should set his employees to work anywhere outside his own house where he might easily supervise their work, and that no fletchers' work should be done at night. All these were, of course, problems that had been at issue when the Fletchers first claimed their independence from the Bowyers, and it is hardly credible that the Company's leading members had not sought to address them in the meantime. Enrolment of the formal ordinances at Guildhall made offences against these regulations directly subject to the adjudication of the mayor and aldermen. The penalties for any infractions were financial, and the fines were divided equally between the Company's and the City's coffers.[27]

It was not until the spring of 1484 that the Fletchers brought a further set of ordinances to Guildhall for approval and enrolment, the Company's most comprehensive set of rules and regulations yet.[28] There was an explicit affirmation of the wardens' authority, both concerning their powers of search and oversight of the manufacture of arrows, but also of the members of the craft and their conduct more generally. Particular sanctions were reserved for the use of 'unfittyng or unmannerly words or langage', both towards the wardens and towards other members of the Company, a concern widely held by urban and company authorities at this time.[29]

---

26   GL, MS 21116; J. Bromley and H. Child, *The Armorial Bearings of the Guilds of London* (London, 1960), pp. vii, xviii–xix, 96–7; I.A. Gadd, '"Ornamental for Closet or House": Printed Catalogues of the Arms of the London Livery Companies, 1596–1677', *The Coat of Arms*, 3rd ser. iii (2007), 55–66, at pp. 55–6. The only known grants of arms earlier than that of the Fletchers are those of the Drapers (1439), Haberdashers (1446), Vintners (1447), Barbers (1451), Pewterers (1451), Girdlers (1454), Ironmongers (1455), Tallowchandlers (1456), Cooks (1461), Glovers (1464), Upholders (1465), and Carpenters (1466).

27   LMA, Letter Book K, ff. 6, 106v, see appendix 2, below, no. 3.

28   It is interesting that the Bowyers, who at this period also did not have their own charter, did not present a comparable set of ordinances until four years later, when they, along with other companies, were ordered to do so by the mayor and aldermen.

29   On the wider concern with contumacious language, see e.g. C.D. Liddy, '"Sir ye be not king": Citizenship and Speech in Late Medieval and Early Modern England', *Historical Journal*, lx (2017), 571–96; *idem*, 'Cultures of Surveillance in Late Medieval English Towns: The Monitoring of Speech and the Fear of Revolt' in *The Routledge History Handbook of Medieval Revolt* ed. J. Firnhaber-Baker and D. Schoenaers (Abingdon, 2017), pp. 311–29.

There were rules for the conduct of the Fletchers' communal affairs: four annual gatherings of the membership were to be held on the four quarter days – the feasts of the Conversion of St. Paul (25 January), St. George (23 April), St. Mary Magdalene (22 July) and the Translation of St. Edward the Confessor (13 October) – while a fifth (the Decollation of St. John the Baptist, on 29 August) was given over to a communal religious celebration. The prohibition of working or trading on Sundays was re-iterated, but in addition there were other more detailed rules for the exercise of the fletcher's trade. The wardens' right to examine the skills of any fletcher wishing to work or trade in the City was affirmed, and fixed rates of pay for workmen in the trade set out. Apprentices completing their training were to be sworn to keep the rules and regulations of the Company. Disputes between members of the Company were in the first instance to be brought before the wardens for settlement, while any members found guilty of serious crimes, such as theft or embezzlement, were to be expelled. Fletchers keeping shops were banned from displaying at any one time more than two sheaves of 'any manere of artelery' (a term used to describe any of the missiles propelled from a hand-held weapon like a bow or crossbow), and, finally, the members of the craft were banned from selling their goods at any fairs and markets held within a 30 mile radius of London, and wares that were to go further afield were first to be inspected by the Company's wardens.[30] The influx of outsiders into the trade was a constant concern of the Fletchers, as it was for most other crafts.[31] The ordinances of 1484 provided that no foreigner or alien might be taken to apprentice or hired as a journeyman unless he had first been examined by the Company's wardens as to his skills. Around 1500, the Fletchers sought to restrict the access of 'foreigners', encompassing anyone who was not a freeman of London, to the City's labour market even further. The Fletchers' wardens apparently first raised the issue in 1501–2 during the mayoralty of Sir John Shaa, and found the mayor receptive to their complaints, but it was only in the following year that they placed a formal ordinance before the mayor and aldermen, under the terms of which members of the craft were not only barred from employing foreigners, if freemen of the City could be found, but also from creating work for fletchers outside the City by selling fletchers' timber in its unworked state to outsiders.[32]

While the formal record of the Fletchers' ordinances in the archives of the Guildhall makes the process of the craft's regulation look smooth and uncontentious, it is clear that the reality was different, and that there

---

30   LMA, Letter Book L, ff. 196v–198.
31   For the wider picture see most recently M.P. Davies, 'Aliens, crafts and guilds in late medieval London', in *Medieval Londoners: Essays to mark the eightieth birthday of Caroline M. Barron* ed. E.A. New and C. Steer (London, 2019), pp. 119–47, at pp. 136–7; S.R. Hovland, 'Apprenticeship in Later Medieval London (c.1300–c.1530)' (Univ. of London Ph.D. thesis, 2006), pp. 177–9.
32   LMA, Journal 10, f. 280v.

was periodic opposition, on however limited a scale, to the rules laid down by the leading men of the Company.[33] The ordinances of 1484 expressly included provisions to quash dissent, laying down a fine of 20*s.* to be imposed (repeatedly, if necessary) on any member of the craft who should 'have any unfitting or slanderous language' potentially prejudicial to the Company's standing, concerning the enactment of any of the Fletchers' other ordinances.[34] Moreover, as in the case of Robert atte Verne in the late fourteenth century, it was not always the more junior and obscure members of the Company who caused problems, but rather older and more established men who perhaps felt themselves to be above censure by the wardens of the day. Little is known of the offence of Richard Holmes of the parish of St. Magnus, other than his eventual formal acknowledgement that he had 'obstinately and inobediently', and on more than one occasion, behaved in an unbecoming manner towards the wardens and masters of the Fletchers and broken the rules and ordinances of both the Company and the City. His disagreement with the Fletchers' wardens was evidently considered no trifling matter, for in December 1517 he was placed in Newgate prison while his case was decided by the mayor and aldermen, but it may nevertheless have amounted to no more than an open refusal to abide by the wardens' direction, and the use of contumacious language. In any event, in January 1518 Holmes humbly submitted to the Company's wardens in a formal ceremony overseen by two aldermen. He died three years later, apparently fully reconciled to his fellow fletchers, since in his will he left bequests of 6*s.* 8*d.* to the Company's liverymen, and 13*s.* 4*d.* to its poor men, in return for their prayers for his soul.[35] Contumacious language

---

33   Beyond the jurisdiction of the Company's wardens or even the city authorities, there were of course, as in all walks of life, instances of outright criminal behaviour by individual fletchers. A prominent example was the fletcher Richard Logeman who in 1462 was accused of having been an accessory to the rape of Elizabeth Venour, wife of William Venour, the warden of the Fleet prison. Logeman enjoyed the distinction of being brought to trial in the court of King's bench before King Edward IV presiding in his own person, something no King had done in living memory, and was eventually granted a full royal pardon (TNA, KB 27/806, rex rot. 3d; KB 9/300, nos. 42–3). Equally publicly, in 1518 the fletcher Henry Rand was found guilty of having perjured himself in the evidence he had given in a dispute between one Hugh Lewis, a Welshman, and the chapman John Purser. Rand was sentenced to be taken through the streets of the City on horseback, facing the horse's tail, wearing on his head a paper with the inscription 'For wylful perjurye', and then to stand under the pillory for half an hour on three successive market days, while his offence was being proclaimed, before being banished from the City. Rand knew what was expected of him, and made a display of his 'grete sorowe and lamentyng', but the haberdasher Thomas Wyggyns who was punished alongside him for the same offence 'toke his seyd penaunce rather in derision and skorne … and shewed hymselff no thing sory thereof but rather made a laughing and sporte therof', for which contumacious behaviour he was physically locked into the pillory by the neck and wrists on the remaining two days of his punishment (LMA, Repertory 3, ff. 263r–v).

34   LMA, Letter Book L, f. 198.

35   Oxley, *Fletchers and Longbowstringmakers*, pp. 17–18; LMA, Repertory 3, ff. 261r–262r;

was held against the fletcher Thomas Smyth when in the summer of 1531 he was referred to the mayor's jurisdiction and threatened with the loss of his freedom of the City.[36] Smyth may have been guilty of offences similar to those with which his namesake and possible kinsman, William Smyth (d.1555) was charged about the same time. William was said to have broken the Company's ordinance of 1503 by selling raw timber to foreigners, and, on his refusal to be ruled by his Company's wardens, had been clapped in prison on the mayor's orders. Smyth maintained in his defence that the draft ordinance of 1503 had never been approved by the mayor and Common Council, and that it had consequently been common practice among the fletchers to deal in such wood. This was an interesting defence, for Smyth had himself served as one of the Fletchers' wardens in 1519, and thus ought to have known better. Yet, by then the events of 1503 lay more than twenty years in the past, and while the passage of the Fletchers' petition was recorded in the repertory of the Court of Aldermen, it was never, it seems, copied into the City's Letter Book, and it may have been on this lacuna that Smyth based his case. In any event, having unsuccessfully appealed to the Chancellor of England, Sir Thomas More, for redress, in the summer of 1531 William, also, made his peace with the Company, and went on to serve two further terms as warden in 1535 and 1544.[37]

The social dimension of the Fletchers' regulations provides an example of the wider role of the companies in the day-to-day government of the pre-modern City. Alongside the clearly defined and delimited units of the ward and the parish, which provided the basic sub-units of civic and ecclesiastical government, each with their specific responsibilities for the regulation of daily life, the companies provided an over-arching system of regulation peculiar to the practitioners of a particular craft or trade, rather than a specific geographical locality.[38] While the City authorities sought to exercise a degree of oversight over the companies' regulation of their members and

---

Repertory 5, ff. 78r, 85r, 86r, 89v; TNA, PROB 11/20, ff. 95v–96r. Holmes was not a poor man: in the early stages of the proceedings against him in October 1517 he was able to lay to pledge a gold chalice and patten, and a diamond ring: Repertory 5, f. 85r.

36 LMA, Repertory 8, f. 165v. Thomas Smyth went on to serve as a warden of the Fletchers' company in 1538. In July 1547, however, he appeared before the court of aldermen and produced witnesses of great age who attested to his admission to the freedom on completing his apprenticeship many years earlier. He himself no longer had a copy of his freedom, nor could any corresponding entry be found in the chamberlain's registers. As he had been recognised as a freeman all his life, had acted as one and had himself presented apprentices for admission, he now sought to have his status regularised, so that this administrative lacuna might not be to the detriment of his former apprentices or his own children, a petition which was granted by the court of aldermen. In return, Smyth gratefully presented the City with six sheaves of arrows in 'mete and apte' cases. LMA, Repertory 11, f. 335v.

37 LMA, Journal 10, f. 277; Repertory 1, f. 121; TNA, C 1/677/17; Repertory 8, ff. 168r–v.

38 For a pioneering study that seeks to cut across the formal boundaries of parish and ward, see J. Colson, 'Local Communities in Fifteenth Century London: Craft, Parish and Neighbourhood' (Univ. of London Ph.D. thesis, 2011).

wherever possible endeavoured to suppress privileges granted to individual companies by the Crown unless they had been expressly sanctioned at Guildhall, they nevertheless recognised the part played by the companies' wardens in the overall rule of the City.[39]

While less rigidly defined than the boundaries of wards and parishes, there was also a loose geographical dimension to the activity of the companies within the City of London, since out of convenience, as much as practicality, the members of individual trades or crafts had tended to concentrate their shops in particular neighbourhoods.[40] In the case of the 'warrior' trades, such an arrangement is readily explained by the close inter-dependence of crafts like fletchers and bowyers, and the manufacturers of the components of their wares, while the existence of a market for their goods in the aristocratic residences clustered to the west of the City may account for the location of one of the early centres of London's fletcher community in and around Bowyer Row to the immediate west of St. Paul's cathedral, in the parish of St. Martin Ludgate.[41] Here, a concentration of fletchers was also still found after their separation from the bowyers. Prominent members of the craft resident there in the fifteenth century included Thomas Prentys (d.1414), warden in 1376, Henry Hoggys (d.1439), warden in 1438, William Crane (d.1440) and his one-time apprentice, Thomas Clarell (d.1445), Roger Daveney (d.1446), warden in 1424, William Water (d.1463), William Logeman (d.1480), and Thomas Kyng (d.1484).[42] A second group of fletchers in this period plied their trade on the western outskirts of the City, in the parishes of St. Bride's Fleet Street, St. Sepulchre without Newgate, St. Dunstan in the West, St. Clement Danes and St. Mary le Strand.[43] During the fifteenth century, a further concentration of fletchers, bowyers and other armouring trades developed on and around the Bridge.[44] In the years after 1405, properties on the Bridge passed into the hands of the fletchers William Warewyk and John Hale, and on the far side of the bridge the fletchers John White, John Beste and Robert Machon

---

39   Rappaport, *Worlds within Worlds*, p. 213.
40   Barron, *London in the Later Middle Ages, 199*; J. Colson, 'Commerce, Clusters, and Community: a Re-evaluation of the Occupational Geography of London, c.1400–c.1550', *Economic History Review*, n.s., lxix (2016), 104–30.
41   D. Keene, 'Metalworking in Medieval London: an Historical Survey', *Historical Metallurgy*, xxx (1996), 95–102, at p. 99.
42   GL, MSS 9171/2, f. 294v; 9171/4, ff. 25, 36, 173, 189v; 9171/5, f. 147; 9171/6, f. 289; 9171/7, f. 3; *CCR*, 1399–1402, p. 362.
43   Examples of early fletchers based in these western parishes include for St. Clement Danes: John Pery, 1455 (TNA, CP 40/776, rot. 329); William Robynson, 1484 (CP 40/890, rot. 66d); Edmund Dolson, 1496 (CP 40/951, rot. 144d). St. Mary le Strand: William Murrey, 1470 (CP 40/837, rot. 16). St. Bride: John Hardekyn (GL, MS 9171/3, f. 362v); John Crane, 1439/43 (GL, MS 9171/4, f. 125v). St. Sepulchre: Thomas Sutton, 1437 (GL, MS 9171/3, f. 489); William Carter, 1444 (GL, MS 9171/4, f. 135Bv). St. Dunstan: Geoffrey Shedburn, 1464 (GL, MS 9171/5, f. 361).
44   Colson, 'Commerce, Clusters, and Community', pp. 119–20.

established themselves in Southwark. Far from being peripheral members of their trade, by the 1480s the fletchers based on the Bridge included leading liverymen like Henry Crane and Henry Felde, the wardens in 1460–1.[45]

One factor that doubtless affected the geographical distribution of London's fletchers was the continuity (or otherwise) of individual businesses from one generation to the next. Among the fletcher 'dynasties' documented in the early period were the Cranes: William Crane (*d*.1440), first recorded in London in 1401, was followed into the trade by his son John (*d*.1443). John was in turn succeeded by his son, Henry, who was appointed King's Fletcher in 1460 and survived until 1486. Crucially, however, John set up his shop in the parish of St. Bride's, whereas his father's shop in St. Martin Ludgate was taken over by the former's apprentice, Thomas Clarell (*d*.1445).[46] In a similar development, on the death of the fractious William Smyth in 1555, one of his houses in Coleman Street (to the south of Glyn Alley) was to pass to his daughter Elizabeth, the wife of the fletcher Thomas Crompe (*d*.1590), warden in 1568 and 1575.[47]

In the shaping of these professional dynasties the wives and widows of London's fletchers played a pivotal role. In many instances, widows took over their husband's shops after their deaths, and it is reasonable to suppose that they had played a part in their running even in their spouses' lifetimes. Before his death in 1545 John Romynge of Holborn bridge (over the Fleet river) explicitly instructed his wife Juliana to pay for his nephew and apprentice (another John Romynge) to be made 'free with the Fletchers' upon completion of his apprenticeship (the implication being that she would also oversee the completion of his training).[48]

It was not uncommon in medieval London for women to play an active part in their husbands' businesses during the former's lives, and also to continue these enterprises after their deaths,[49] but the practice seems to

45 By virtue of the survival of regularly renewed rentals, the property belonging to the wardens of London Bridge is exceptionally well documented: *London Bridge: Selected Accounts and Rentals, 1381–1538*, ed. V. Harding and L. Wright (London Record Society xxxi, 1995), nos. 132, 136, 137; LMA, Bridge Accounts 3, ff. 1r, 20r–v, 65r–v, 83r, 322r–v; Bridge Accounts 4, ff. 2r–v. Later residents in the parish of St. Magnus by the Bridge included Richard Otehill, 1457, warden of the Fletchers in 1420 (GL, MS 9171/5, f. 198); Walter Hende, 1519 (TNA, PROB 11/19, ff. 114v–115); William Temple, 1535 (TNA, CP 40/1084, rot 635d); John Starky and John Wilshire, both 1541 (*The Acts and Monuments of John Foxe*, ed. S.R. Cattley (8 vols., London, 1838–41), v. 444); John Wardall, 1580, in a property known as the 'Three tonnes' (GL, MS 9051/4, f. 194v); and John Bassett (TNA, C 1/1333/19). Among the fletchers renting property on the Bridge in the second half of fifteenth century were John Abynden, John Curate, Gilbert Forman, Robert Goldsmyth, Robert Haldenby, William Love, William Motte, Richard Payn and Nicholas Roblesse: LMA, Bridge Accounts 3, ff. 1r, 20r–v, 65r–v, 83r, 322r–v; Bridge Accounts 4, ff. 2r–v.
46 GL, MS 9171/4, ff. 125v–126.
47 GL, MS 9171/13, f. 58v.
48 TNA, PROB 11/30, f. 192.
49 C.M. Barron, 'The "Golden Age" of Women in Medieval London', in *Women in Southern*

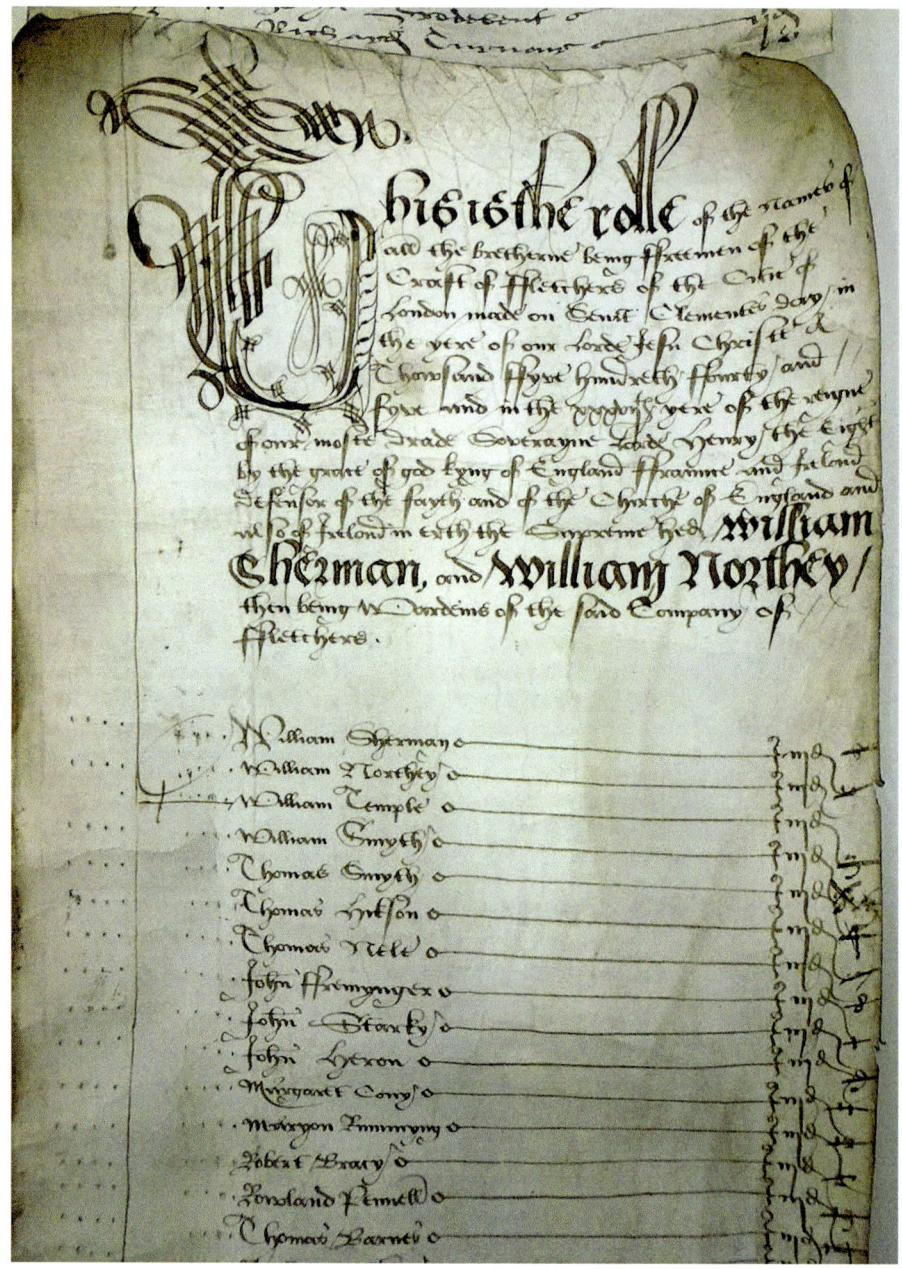

FIG. 3: Quarterage roll of the Fletchers' Company, 1545–6. Among the members named are the widows Marion Romynge and Margaret Cony. Guildhall Library, London, MS 5977/1, m. 12. © Worshipful Company of Fletchers. Photograph: John Leatherdale.

have been particularly common among the Fletchers. Named fletchers who supplied arrows to the royal arsenal at the Tower of London in the reign of Edward III were Alice Flour, Alice Russel and Alice Drogman,[50] and the Company's early quarterage registers regularly show widows assuming their husbands' places on the latter's deaths. By the 1560s, when these lists began to separate out the leading Fletchers as 'masters', separate sections for the 'widows' were also introduced. In some instances, these fletcher widows make only a brief appearance, perhaps continuing payments to the Company only while winding up their husbands' affairs, but in other cases it seems clear that they continued to run fletching businesses in their own right, and sometimes for prolonged periods. Perhaps the most remarkable example was Margaret, the widow of Thomas Cony. Thomas, who had been warden of the Fletchers' Company in 1525 and died in the late spring of 1527, was a man of some substance. At his death he owned lands in Hertfordshire and Middlesex, and leased others in Southwark and Newington, and the witnesses to his will included two leading members of his craft, William Temple and John Wilshire. Margaret was his second wife, a first one, Agnes, having predeceased him, and it is likely that she was some years younger than he. He nevertheless appointed her, as was not unusual in London, as his executrix alongside his brother, William. Margaret first appeared in the Fletchers' registers in the year of her husband's death, and thereafter was listed for more than thirty years until 1559, when she may herself have died.[51] Nor was Margaret Cony unique in her extensive career. Other widows who paid their quarterage for long periods of years included Joan, widow of John Young, from 1513 to 1521, Margaret, widow of Richard Holmes, recorded from 1521 to 1529; Helen, widow of John Kylby, from 1583 to 1594, and Joan, widow of John Wardall from 1580 to 1590.[52]

How full a part these women played in the life of the Company is hard to fathom, but it is perhaps instructive that Joan Wardall, whose name appears on the Fletchers' quarterage lists for ten years after her husband's death wished the members of the Company to attend her funeral, and made provision for a communal meal by way of a wake,[53] while Elizabeth, widow of William Sherman (*d*.1570), at least four time a warden between 1537 and 1560, not only disappeared from the Fletchers' lists within less than

England (Reading Medieval Studies xv, 1989), 35–58, and also see the introduction to *Medieval London Widows, 1300–1500*, ed. C.M. Barron and A.F. Sutton (London, 1994). For individual examples the essays within the same collection, and also A.F. Sutton, *Wives and Widows of Medieval London* (Donington, 2016).

50 T. Richardson, *The Tower Armoury in the Fourteenth Century* (Leeds, 2016), p. 113. Richardson's reference to Oxley is spurious.

51 TNA, PROB 11/22, f. 146r–v; GL, MS 5977/1, mm. 3–8; 5977/2, m. 1; Worcestershire Archive and Archaeology Service, Berington MSS, 705:24/266.

52 GL, MS 5977/1–2, *passim*.

53 GL, MSS 9051/4, f. 195; 9171/17, f. 297v.

two years of her husband's death, but on her own demise in 1574 provided a 'recreation' for the Painter-Stainers, rather than the company in which Sherman had been so prominent.[54]

Indeed, if the economic and personal independence that the control of a commercial enterprise gave to London widows in the later middle ages has caused some modern scholars to consider the period a 'golden age' for women,[55] the reality could be rather less romantic. A widow owning a profitable business represented an attractive target for prospective suitors, and a remarriage, that handed control of her affairs to a second husband, could sometimes be disastrous for her fletcher's business and those associated with it, including, in some instances, the hapless woman herself. This was the case with Elizabeth, the widow of the fletcher John Jones. On Jones's death, Elizabeth had taken on the running of his business, and the instruction of an apprentice. Within a short period of time, however, she had remarried, and had taken as her new husband the skinner Richard Cook. Although Cook gained admission to the Fletchers' Company, he continued to work as a skinner, and hired journeymen to run his wife's workshop. It is possible that Cook was a particularly nasty piece of work: he was accused not only of beating and maltreating his wife's apprentice, Oliver Rande (or Randys), and several of his other servants, both men and women, but even the by now elderly Elizabeth herself.[56]

54   GL, MS 9051/4, f. 49.

55   Barron, "'Golden Age'", *passim*, and see some of the earlier literature cited by Barron, but see also contrary or qualified views set out by e.g. J. Bennett, "'History That Stands Still': Women's Work in the European Past', *Feminist Studies*, xiv (1988), 269–83; M.F. Stevens, 'London Women, the Courts and the "Golden Age": A Quantitative Analysis of Female Litigants in the Fourteenth and Fifteenth Centuries', *The London Journal*, xxxvii (2012), 67–88.

56   TNA, C 1/70/145; C 1/107/27.

The Fletchers' Craft

The fletcher, concerned principally with the flights and shafts of arrows and crossbow bolts (or quarrels), worked mainly in wood and feathers. The manufacture of the different kinds of arrow heads required was, by contrast, the preserve of a separate group of craftsmen, the arrowhead makers, whose noisier workshops by the late fifteenth and early sixteenth centuries appear to have been concentrated in the extramural parish of St. Mary le Strand.[57] The requirements of the fletchers' craft, by contrast, are apparent from the bequest that Richard Parkyns (or Parkynson) left to his apprentice Edward Armstrong in 1558, presumably to start him off in business in his own right:

> '... of long seasoned timber seven hundred of birch and seven hundred of asp, and short seasoned timber one and a half thousand; his best plane; twelve of his best shaves; a nock saw and a slit saw, and his best pair of shears and 20s. in money...'.[58]

'Fletcher's timber' was among the most common bequests left to younger relatives or apprentices who were presumably expected to set up with their own shops, and while Parkynson was unusual in listing the tools of his trade, other fletchers also made comparable bequests. In 1484 Thomas Kyng left his apprentice Thomas Water not only two thousands of timber, but also a thousand of goose feathers and half a thousand of swan feathers; in 1520 Richard Holmes stipulated that after his death six thousands of fletchers' timber were to be divided between his three apprentices Hugh, Richard and Stephen, once they had completed the terms of the apprenticeship;

---

57 Early known representatives of this craft resident in that parish include Thomas Playter (1480), Humphrey Wellys (bef. 1526), and Robert Wharton (bef. 1536): TNA, CP 40/871, rots. 62, 352d; CP 40/1049, rot. 644; CP 40/1088, rot. 665; CP 40/1092, rot. 338.

58 TNA, PROB 11/42A/117. Armstrong occurs in the Fletchers' company's quarterage list along with his former master's widow in 1560: GL, MS 5977/2, m. 2.

and a thousand of fletcher's timber was assigned in 1545 by John Romynge to John Phylypp.[59]

It is clear that seasoned wood of a superior quality was required to make arrow shafts, and the quantities in which this raw material was required were such that there were woodmongers who specialised in supplying this particular commodity. In 1426, John Howton, one such trader, expressly styled himself a 'timberman of fletchers' timber'. Naturally, Howton maintained close connexions among the City's fletchers: when he made his will in the same year, he appointed Reynold Kyrton, citizen and fletcher, the overseer of his executors.[60] Moreover, the supply of good quality timber continued to be a central concern of the Fletchers' wardens into the sixteenth century. The use of poor or insufficiently dried wood had been outlawed in the Company's early ordinances, and although an attempt by the wardens also to ban the sale of 'unwrought' wooden shafts to non-Londoners had been rejected by the mayor and aldermen in 1502–3, the Fletchers' officers continued to press the point. As we have seen, in about 1530 William Smyth, himself a former warden of the Fletchers, complained to the Chancellor of having been arrested on precisely these grounds, even though the prohibition had never been approved at Guildhall, the City authorities having taken the wardens' word at face value, without checking their own records.[61]

Something of the fletcher's work is apparent from the rates of pay laid down in the Company ordinances of 1484:

'That all such persons ... within the said craft shall have and take from henceforth for their labour for the workmanship and making of these things underwritten after the rate ensuing, that is to say:

For the making of 100 'beryngshaftes' of seasoned timber, well and cleanly made, cross-nocked, skinned and seared – 14d.

---

59   GL, MS 9171/7, f. 3; TNA, PROB 11/20, f. 96; PROB 11/30, f. 192. Phylypp's relationship to Romynge is not otherwise specified. He may have been a journeyman or former apprentice: a man of this name occurs in the Fletchers' quarterage lists from 1536. This man who resided at Temple Bar was named among the Company's masters by 1566 and served as warden in 1572–3. He died in 1574, and was for a time succeeded in the Company's ranks by his widow, who had, however, abandoned the trade and the Company by 1577: GL, MSS 9171/16, f 184v; 5977/1, mm. 7–12; 5977/2, mm. 1–11.

60   GL, MS 9171/3, f. 179. On woodmongers, who in their majority seem to have been engaged in supplying firewood and building timber, see the discussion in J.A. Galloway, D. Keene and M. Murphy, 'Fuelling the City: Production and Distribution of Firewood and Fuel in London's Region, 1290–1400', *Economic History Review*, n.s., xlix (1996). 447–72, pp. 452–3.

61   TNA, C 1/677/17.

For making of 100 of the best 'beryngshaftes', well and cleanly cross-nocked after the best manner and skinned and seared, as is aforesaid – 16*d*.

For the making of 100 'merkearroweshaftes', well and cleanly made after the form aforesaid – 20*d*.

For the making of 100 bolts, well and cleanly made after the best form and after the manner above rehearsed – [–].'[62]

The emphasis in these rates of pay was clearly on the mass production of arrows. The later middle ages were a period of semi-permanent warfare, in which the growing importance of the archer armed with the long-bow created a heightened demand for war arrows. The fletcher whose shop could produce this commodity in significant quantities was thus assured a market for his wares.[63] In the seven years from 1344 to 1351 the keeper of the Privy Wardrobe in the Tower responsible for purchases of armaments, Robert Mildenhall, recorded purchases in London of no fewer than 37,163 sheaves of arrows (some 891,912 arrows).[64] If the formal (if temporary) end of the warfare on the continent in 1453 undoubtedly had an impact on the economic fortunes of the London fletchers, the domestic battles of the Wars of the Roses that followed may to some extent have offset this. Although many of the armaments of the provincial levies that fought in these engagements were undoubtedly sourced in the localities,[65] London continued to act as an assembly point particularly for armies equipped by the government of the day. Thus, for instance, forces set out from the capital to the battles of Northampton (1460), St. Albans (1461) and Barnet (1471), but also to engagements further afield: in the spring of 1461 the Fletchers' wardens (Henry Crane and Henry Felde) provided arrows to a total value

---

62 LMA, Letter Book L, f. 196v. It is likely that in keeping with general wage trends in the later middle ages these rates were rather higher than those that had been paid a century earlier, and certainly higher than those paid before the Black Death of the mid fourteenth century, when labour had been in more plentiful supply: D. Woodward, 'Wage Rates and Living Standards in Pre-Industrial England', *Past and Present*, xci (1981), 28–46; C. Dyer with A.C. Penn, 'Wages and Earnings in Late Medieval England: Evidence from the Enforcement of the Labour Laws', *Economic History Review*, n.s. xliii (1990), 356–76.

63 In the 1360s the royal armoury in the Tower handled not merely thousands but sometimes tens of thousands of sheaves of arrows and arrowshafts: Richardson, *Tower Armoury*, p. 112. Not all of these were procured in London, but even a proportion of them would have guaranteed work for large numbers of London fletchers.

64 Richardson, *Tower Armoury*, p. 113, citing TNA, E 372/198, rot. 35, m. 1.

65 In May 1461 Edward IV ordered the payment to the wardens of the Bowyers' company of York of £19 12*s*. for bows they had provided to him: TNA, E 159/240, *brevia directa baronibus* Mich. rot. 1d.

of £14 16s. 4d. for the army that was to march to the battlefield of Towton under the newly acclaimed King Edward IV.[66]

Moreover, as the centre of the English trade in luxury goods, London also provided a market for higher-quality arrows intended for ostentatious display; arrows bound with gold, and using higher quality feathers, rather than the more common goose and swan. An inventory of the archery equipment owned by Sir John Dynham of Nutwell (near Exeter) in Devon in 1422, a wealthy landowner renowned for his shopping trips to London, describes such arrows:

> 'First a dozen of peacock arrows newly bound in two places with gold and silk and with nocks of white horn, headed with spearheads; and a dozen of new peacock arrows with nocks of white horn, laid in three places with gold foil in the feathers, headed with spearheads; ... and twenty-four shafts of white goose, bound with gold and red silk, and 48 shafts of white goose bound with red and black silk, all of one kind; ... and a dozen of peacock arrows with nocks of black horn, bound with gold and red and black silk, headed with duckbills; and four broad hooked arrows of peacock laid in the feathers all with gold foil, ...'

Altogether, the Dynham armoury contained some 600 arrows, about half of them described as old or worn – thus demonstrating that high-quality arrows at least were not regarded as consumables, but were carefully preserved for repeated use – and a number of crossbow bolts.[67]

It is more difficult to put a sales price on these items, but in 1360 the Crown paid 17d. per sheaf of arrows, about three farthings per arrow, and about the same value was placed in 1394 on three hundred arrows listed among the weapons carried by an armed gang, which were altogether valued at 20s. By comparison, the bows carried by the same band of men were said to be worth 2s. a piece. In 1475, two sheaves of arrows found among the goods of the lawyer John Glyn were valued at 4s., a penny a piece.[68] Perhaps in the category of Sir John Dynham's gold-adorned arrows were those taken from the house of Thomas Wyke, a Lancastrian retainer, at Bromham in Bedfordshire in July 1460, which were priced at 2d. a piece,[69]

---

66   TNA, E 159/238, *brevia directa baronibus* Hil. rot. 16d. A number of arrowheads have been recovered from the Towton battlefield, although it is impossible to be certain whether these were of London or regional provenance: T. Sutherland, 'Conflicts and Allies: Historic Battlefields as Multidisciplinary Hubs – A Case Study from Towton AD 1461', *Arms and Armour*, ix (2012), 40–53, at pp. 45–7; idem, 'The bloody battle of Towton, England' in *The Archaeology of Medieval Europe, Vol. 2: Twelfth to Sixteenth Centuries* ed. M. Carver and J. Klapste (Aarhus, 2011), pp. 272–6.

67   Cornwall RO, Arundell MSS, AR 37/34.

68   *CCR*, 1360–64, pp. 10–11; TNA, KB 27/859, rex rot. 11.

69   TNA, KB 27/808, rex rot. 32.

and clearly also of higher quality were the 12 sheaves of arrows purchased by William Worsley, dean of St. Paul's, in 1481, when he set out in the company of King Edward IV on his expedition against the Scots, at a cost of 34s. 8d. (just under 3s. a sheaf or about 1½d. per arrow).[70] Unless the guard of the Tudor Kings was likewise equipped with weapons designed as much for display as for fighting, prices had perhaps increased by 1495, when 110 sheaves of arrows were bought by the captain of Henry VII's guard at the price of 5s. per sheaf, while the accompanying 110 bows were priced at 3s. 4d. each.[71]

Allowing that over and above the rates of pay laid down in the Company ordinances a master running a fletcher's workshop had to find raw materials and fuel, as well as his apprentices' and journeymen's board and lodging, the margin of profit to be made looks rather less generous than might at first sight appear. There can be no doubt that many of London's fletchers, particularly those operating small household-based workshops, if not on the bread line, were far from wealthy, and in the period before 1519, when the Fletchers' Company's quarterage lists begin to survive, their names are often only known from the records of litigation, brought – as often as not – against, rather than by them.

On the other hand, some of the leading men of the craft could make a good deal of money in the course of their careers, even if they could not hope to compete with the City's merchant princes, the mercers, grocers, drapers and so on who traded luxury goods overseas on a grand scale. While the members of all the armouring trades were to some extent hamstrung in their enterprises by the Crown's blanket prohibition on the export of weapons and armour, there was nevertheless a lucrative market to be found in the English garrison of Calais, that could be accessed with special permission: at various times between 1398 and 1402 export licences for quantities of crossbow bolts were granted to the fletchers Stephen Seder and William Crane.[72]

A leading fletcher might gain appointment to the post of King's Fletcher. Documented by the 1320s, and a Household office with its own accommodation in the Tower of London, by the fifteenth century the office was normally held by a London craftsman.[73] The workshop in the Tower was different from those of other fletchers in the City in that it worked exclusively for the King, but it nevertheless formed an integral part of the world of the fletchers of London, by whom it was staffed, and from whom

---

70 *The Estate and Household Accounts of William Worsley, Dean of St. Paul's Cathedral, 1479–1496*, ed. H. Kleineke and S.R. Hovland (London Record Society, 2004), p. 54.

71 A. Hewerdine, *The Yeomen of the Guard and the Early Tudors: The Formation of a Royal Bodyguard* (London, 2012), p. 30.

72 *CCR*, 1396–9, p. 337; *CCR*, 1399–1402, pp. 342, 535, 554.

73 M. Mercer, 'King's Armourers and the Growth of the Armourer's Craft in Early Fourteenth-Century London', in *Fourteenth Century England VIII*, ed. J.S. Hamilton (Woodbridge, 2014), pp. 1–20, at p. 11; Megson, 'Bowyers', p. 5.

TABLE: King's Fletchers, 1440–1560

Date of appointment	Name	Reference	Comments
6 Mar. 1440	John Frampton	*CPR*, 1441–6, p. 442; *CPR*, 1446–52, p. 523	warden 1441–2
5 Dec. 1460 (confirmed Oct. 1461)	Henry Crane	*CPR*, 1452–61, p. 644; *CPR*, 1461–7, p. 52; TNA, E 159/240, *brevia directa baronibus* Hil. rots. 3, 10	warden 1460–1 *d*.1486
22 Oct. 1486	William Lovell	*CPR*, 1485–94, p. 33	
27 Dec. 1494	John Young	*CPR*, 1494–1509, p. 10	*d*.1513
23 May 1509	Walter Hende	*LP Hen. VIII*, i. 94(21)	*d*.1519
15 Sept. 1518	William Temple	*LP Hen. VIII*, ii. 4434	warden 1527–8; *d*.1546
30 May 1549	John Starky	*CPR*, 1548–9, p. 243	*d.c.*1570
8 Oct. 1556	John Smyth	*CPR*, 1555–7, p. 360	warden 1568–9, 1577–8; *d*.1583
21 June 1560	Starky and Smyth in survivorship	*CPR*, 1558–60, p. 440	

additional supplies of arrows and materials could be and were purveyed.[74] It is thus perhaps not surprising that a number of King's (and Queen's) Fletchers held office as wardens of the London Fletchers: John Frampton in 1441, William Temple in 1527, and John Smyth in 1568 and 1577. Such connexions may have allowed the periodic impressment of fletchers, for which the London workshops presented an obvious target, to be conducted on a more consensual basis than might otherwise have been the case.[75]

Conversely, the King's Fletcher and his staff could be required to leave the comforts of home and accompany the monarch's entourage when he went to war. Thus, for instance, in February 1430 William Crane was instructed to recruit and procure in London, as well as elsewhere, fletchers and workmen, as well as supplies of silk, wax, feathers and fletchers' timber,

---

74   *LP Hen. VIII*, i. 1463 (viii).

75   For the impressment of fletchers, arrowsmiths and other craftsmen for work in the Tower, see e.g. B. Kirkland, '"Now thrive the Armourers": The Development of the Armourers' Crafts and the Forging of Fourteenth-century London' (Univ. of York D.Phil. thesis, 2015), pp. 213–14, 218–19; *CPR*, 1422–9, p. 122; *CPR*, 1446–52, p. 335; *CPR*, 1485–94, pp. 258, 359.

for the young Henry VI's coronation expedition to France.[76]

In times of war, the scale of the operation headed by the King's Fletcher was vast: in March 1514, Walter Hende acknowledged the receipt from John Bayly, a 'hardwareman' of Sheffield of no fewer than 180,012 'lyverey heddes'.[77] But at other times, too, the office was desirable. Even outside the periods of open warfare, the Crown purchased arrows in substantial quantities, and, where ceremonial display was intended, evidently of superior quality. In 1496 and 1499, John Young respectively provided 100 and 70 sheaves of arrows, along with the requisite quivers and girdles, for the King's guard, while in 1519 William Temple was ordered to supply 109 sheaves with cases and girdles.[78] Moreover, the office brought with it daily wages of 6d. (amounting to an annual salary of more than £9), and a livery robe of the type worn by the yeomen of the King's chamber, renewed once a year.[79]

---

76   *CPR*, 1429–36, p. 44. On the expedition of 1430 more generally, see A.E. Curry, 'The "Coronation Expedition" and Henry VI's court in France, 1430–1432', in *The Lancastrian Court*, ed. J. Stratford (Donington, 2003), pp. 29–52.

77   *LP Hen. VIII*, i. 2832 (iv).

78   Hewerdine, *Yeomen of the Guard*, pp. 54–5.

79   TNA, E 159/243, *brevia directa baronibus* Hil. rot. 16d.

The Social and Geographical Origins of the Fletchers

Perhaps one of the most obscure aspects of the early history of the London Fletchers' Company is the origin of its members. In some instances, as we have seen, members of established fletching families continued in the trade. The sons (and perhaps also daughters) of fletchers probably received their initial instruction at their father's (or mother's) knee, but may then often have been apprenticed to another member of the Company, although the information available on the majority of the Company's apprentices in the early period means that it is only rarely possible to establish their parentage and origins. Overall, the available evidence is too anecdotal to allow for any general conclusions, beyond the observation that the fletcher's craft was no different from others in drawing men to the capital from all over England. Some came from the City's hinterland, like Thomas Kyng (*d*.1484), whose father Richard lived in Maidstone in Kent,[80] Edward Nelson, son of a man from Great Warley in Essex, or Thomas Taillor, whose parents came from Rotherhithe in Surrey. Others hailed from further afield, like John Blake who came from Warwickshire, Robert Bayley (*d*.1572) from Lincolnshire, and John Reve the elder from Nottinghamshire. If any particular region was heavily represented, it was perhaps Wales and its marches: John Reve the younger and John Harrolde originated in Gloucestershire, John Cock (or Cox) in Herefordshire, Thomas Salte (*d.c*.1583) in Staffordshire, and along with John ap Rice (or Price) and Roger Eton there were in the sixteenth century a number of fletchers with Welsh names like ap Howell (or Powell), Gryffin (or Gryffith) or Jones in the Company's ranks. The apprentice fletchers enrolled in the mid sixteenth century rarely came from families of substance, frequently giving their father's profession as 'husbandmen'

---

80   *CCR*, 1468–76, no. 1100.

(the lowest rank of agricultural householder recognised in the period), or else as weavers, shoemakers, carpenters or minstrels.[81]

Some craftsmen had trained elsewhere, and came to London in search of commercial opportunities. They may have included John Watson, recorded from 1519 and 1527, and from 1525 to 1527 referred to as 'of Bury', or Richard Hert and Richard Cook who throughout the period of their respective inclusion in the Company's quarterage lists from 1521 to 1525, and 1525 to 1527, were described as 'of Exeter'.[82] Towards the end of the sixteenth century, a number of the Company's members were explicitly styled 'foreigners', that is, Englishmen, but not citizens of London, men such as John Pyme (d.1590), Edward Varnam (fl.1600/02), Thomas Child (d.1602), and Robert Peacock (d.1594).[83] By contrast, there is little evidence to substantiate the fears of outsiders displacing Englishmen in the workforce expressed in the ordinances of 1484: the records of a tax imposed on aliens a year earlier, in 1483, records just a single man born overseas in the household of a London fletcher, the German Thomas Wale, a servant to Henry Crane.[84]

The training of the fletchers' apprentices, like that in other crafts and trades, was governed by the City of London's regulations. The names of apprentices were recorded at Guildhall, and on successful completion of their terms, by City custom set at a minimum of seven years (but upwardly variable depending on the apprentice's skill), they could petition for admission to the freedom of the City.[85] It was expected that masters would train their apprentices in their craft, but, depending on their age and level of knowledge, they might also arrange for them to go to school to learn the rudiments of reading and writing.[86] Considerable emphasis was naturally placed on the learning of the craft itself: many disputes that came before the authorities concerned masters accused of setting their apprentices menial tasks, such as the minding of horses or the 'carrying of a child in sheets', while in 1366 an apprentice draper complained that his master had made

---

81   *Register of Freemen of the City of London in the Reigns of Henry VIII and Edward VI*, ed. C. Welch (London and Middlesex Archaeological Society, 1908), pp. 11, 16, 44, 58, 92, 104.

82   GL, MS 5977/1, mm. 2–5. Richard Hert had been admitted to the freedom of Exeter by redemption in September 1514, and presumably returned to that city when he disappears from the ranks of the London Company, as he was presenting apprentices for admission to the freedom there as late as 1552. Richard Cook only became a freeman of Exeter in 1529–30, after he disappears from the London records, and like Hert on payment of an entry fine of £1. *Exeter Freemen, 1266–1967*, ed. M.M. Rowe and A.M. Jackson (Exeter, Devon and Cornwall Record Society extra ser. i, 1973), pp. 67, 71, 74.

83   GL, MS 5977/2, mm. 15–20, 22–24.

84   *The Alien Communities of London in the Fifteenth Century: The Subsidy Rolls of 1440 and 1483–4*, ed. J.L. Bolton (Stamford, 1998), p. 55, n. 46.

85   Hovland, 'Apprenticeship', pp. 87–8.

86   *Ibid.*, pp. 96–7.

him work 'as if he were a house boy'.[87] Both direct instruction by the master and the observation of his work and that of experienced journeymen had their part to play, and the absence of this was one of the complaints of Oliver Rande, the unfortunate apprentice of the fletcher John Jones, who complained that after his master's death his mistress's new husband, the skinner Richard Cook, had left him to 'sit in the shopp alone, throff the which he lesith his teching and his informacion'.[88]

Such complaints were in the first instance referred to the wardens of the company concerned, but, if their attempt at a settlement failed could be brought to Guildhall. In Oliver Rande's case, the award of the wardens and City chamberlain that the apprentice might be released from his indentures if he paid Cook 26s. 8d., was repudiated by the master who demanded no less than £40, and had the boy clapped in prison, forcing the apprentice to seek redress in the King's courts. Of Rande's eventual fate nothing is known, but if he completed his training under another master, he does not subsequently appear to have established himself in the London Fletchers' Company.[89]

While conflicts between master and apprentice make for good stories, it is reasonable to suppose that they represented the exception rather than the rule, and that by and large relations between master fletchers and their apprentices were professional, if not outright cordial. Certainly, bequests to apprentices made by fletchers in their wills, suggest a concern for their welfare, and perhaps outright affection. Some testators made small bequests of money or goods to named individuals.[90] In some instances, one or two favoured apprentices would be left tools and materials, perhaps so they might continue their master's business, or establish their own.[91] In other cases, apprentices might be released from part of the contracted term of their apprenticeship,[92] while in yet others there was provision for apprentices to continue their training under their widowed mistress, or with 'an honest man of the craft', as John Wilshire specified in 1543.[93] Thus, in the 1550s John Harrolde, apprentice to Thomas Smyth, completed his training under his master's widow, Elizabeth, and John Blake did likewise under Agnes, widow of his original master Ralph Reyborne (or Rathbone). Edward Nelson served first under Nicholas Stone, before being committed to the care of Thomas Sherman, and John Reve the younger passed from Thomas Smyth's workshop into that of William Chaloner.[94]

---

87   *Ibid.*, pp. 95–6.
88   TNA, C 1/107/27.
89   TNA, C 1/107/27; Hovland, 'Apprenticeship', pp. 132–3.
90   GL, MSS 9171/3, f. 331; 9171/11, ff. 95v–96; TNA, PROB 11/17, f. 178v.
91   TNA, PROB 11/20, ff. 95v–96r ; PROB 11/52, ff. 197v-198r; GL, MS 9171/7, ff. 3r–v; MS 9171/11, ff. 95v–96; MS 9171/15, f. 350v.
92   TNA, PROB 11/52, ff. 197v-198r.
93   GL, MS 9171/11, f. 96r.
94   Register of Freemen, ed. Welch, pp. 92, 104.

There is a suggestion that some fletchers were in the habit of taking on large numbers of apprentices at any one time: so, for instance, at the time of his death in 1513 John Young had five apprentices (John Copsale, John Hardyng, Henry Knyght, Thomas Nicollis and Anthony Laynard) training under him,[95] and in 1558 Richard Parkynson remembered in his will not only Edward Armstrong, but also two other apprentices, John Shawe and William, to whom he left 13s. 4d. 'so that they may please their mistress'. In parallel, many master fletchers evidently employed journeymen. This is probably indicative of the working patterns of the craft: as arrows and crossbow bolts were mass-produced, cheap labour was at a premium, and once an apprentice had achieved a basic competence, he could be expected to provide this at the cost of his upkeep for the remainder of his term.[96] This did not pose a problem while the demand for arrows remained high. By 1572, however, competition had evidently stiffened, and the Company decided to limit the amount of cheap labour any one master could draw upon by restricting the number of apprentices kept by any current or former warden to two, and by any other master to just a single one.[97]

---

95   TNA, PROB 11/17, f. 178v.
96   Hovland, 'Apprenticeship', p. 100.
97   Oxley, *Fletchers and Longbowstringmakers*, p. 31, and see Appendix 2, no. 7, below.

Communal activities

Even in its earliest guise, a livery company was more than a mere craft organisation exercising oversight over its members' commercial activities. Through the Company's communal conduct of its business the membership gained a collective identity that, not least, gave the individual member a visible status which exceeded that to which he or she might lay claim in his or her own right. The Fletchers' ordinances of 1484 laid down that its members would gather four times a year, on the feasts of the Conversion of St. Paul (25 January), St. George (23 April), St. Mary Magdalene (22 July) and the Translation of St. Edward the Confessor (13 October), for quarterly meetings at which the craft's affairs would be discussed. These business meetings aside, there were also other occasions on which the Fletchers might gather as a body.

In their early incarnations, the craft guilds of medieval London were religious in nature, associations of the members of a particular trade or craft for mutual prayer and worship. Central to this, as to much of pre-Reformation religious life, was the doctrine of Purgatory which stipulated that the soul of a deceased Christian would spend a period of time in a state of suspension before moving on to the afterlife in either heaven or hell. The length of time spent in Purgatory was undefined, if calculated in thousands of years. It could, however, be shortened by the purchase during the individual's lifetime of indulgences granting remission of terms of years, by charitable works performed on behalf of the deceased after his or her death, or by intercessory prayer for his or her soul, and it was above all the latter that a communal organisation like a fraternity or company could provide. In this, the prayers of the poor were deemed particularly efficacious, and it was with this in mind that in 1520 Richard Holmes assigned 6s. 8d. to the 'maisters of the felaship of flechers of London being in the clothing', but 13s. 4d. to 'the poore men of the same felaship being out of clothyng', specifying that the latter were to pray for his soul.[98]

---

98 TNA, PROB 11/20, f. 96r. On the doctrine of Purgatory, see C. Burgess, "'A Fond Thing

FIG. 4: Panoramic View of London from the South Bank (detail), c.1616, by C.J. Visscher, showing the prominent spire of the Austin Friars (then the Dutch Church). © London Metropolitan Archives (City of London).

There is limited evidence of the collective spiritual life of the Fletchers' Company in this earlier period. Where some of the larger companies had associated with them major religious fraternities (such as, for instance, the Merchant Taylors' fraternity of St. John the Baptist), individual fletchers left bequests to various fraternities based in the parishes where they resided. Perhaps on account of the dispersion of the Fletchers in the various parishes of London, the Company's spiritual life centred on a religious house, the Austin friary in Broad Street, not far from the Company hall.[99] It was at the friary that the Fletchers observed their annual feast day, that of the Decollation of St. John the Baptist (29 August), and here the Company also maintained a light, towards which each member annually had to pay 2*d*. It is possible that it was also here that an annual obit for deceased members of the Company was originally held. After the Austin friary's dissolution, the Fletchers had to find an alternative venue, and until the suppression of such practices in 1548 the annual commemoration of the dead was held in the parish church of St. Mary Axe, even closer to the Fletchers' Hall, at an annual cost of 4*s*. – a modest sum, but still twice as much as was annually paid in rent for the hall.[100] There is no concrete evidence to show what

Vainly Invented": An essay on Purgatory and Pious Motive in late medieval England', in *Parish, Church and People: Local Studies in Lay Religion, 1350–1750*, ed. S.J. Wright (1988), pp. 56–84; *idem*, '"Longing to be prayed for": Death and Commemoration in an English Parish in the Late Middle Ages', in *The Place of the Dead: Death and Remembrance in Late Medieval and Early Modern Europe*, ed. B. Gordon and P. Marshall (Cambridge, 2000), pp. 44–65.

99   The Austin Friars is one of the better documented of London's medieval friaries. See most recently N. Holder, *The Friaries of Medieval London from Foundation to Dissolution* (Woodbridge, 2017), pp. 119–41 and passim, based on the same author's doctoral thesis 'The Medieval Friaries of London. A Topographic and Archaeological History, Before and After the Dissolution' (Univ. of London Ph.D. thesis, 2011); N. Holder, M. Samuel and I. Betts, 'The Church and Cloisters of Austin Friars', *Transactions of the London and Middlesex Archaeological Society*, lxiv (2013), 143–62; C. Thomas and B. Watson, with J. Bowsher, 'The Mendicant Houses of Medieval London: An Archaeological Review', in *The Friars in Medieval Britain*, ed. N. Rogers (Donington, Harlaxton Medieval Studies, n.s. xix, 2010), pp. 265–97, at pp. 279–81; and also the older account by W.A. Cater, 'The Priory of Austin Friars, London', *Journal of the British Archaeological Association*, xviii (1912), 25–44, 57–82; *The Victoria County History: London*, i. 510–13. The Fletchers were not the only company to gather at the Austin friary; among those known to have done so in the later fifteenth century were also the Pewterers and the Pouchmakers: Holder, *Friaries of Medieval London*, pp. 120, 139; TNA, LR 15/12.

100 The obit was not mentioned in the Company's ordinances, but in 1550 was associated with the name of Henry Felde, one of the wardens in 1460–1, who died in 1486. Felde was a parishioner of St. Magnus, and his will made no explicit mention of an anniversary to be kept for him by the Fletchers, so it is possible that his name was among the first of a longer bede roll (a list of past members to be prayed for) of Fletchers annually commemorated at St. Mary Axe. In July 1550 the Fletchers' annual payment of 4*s*. formed part of the rents and revenues relating to chantries and commemorations that were purchased by the City from the Crown. *London and Middlesex Chantry Certificate, 1548*, ed. C.J. Kitching (London Record Society xvi, 1980), no. 208; *CPR*, 1549–51, p. 396; TNA, E 159/238, *brevia directa* Hil. rot. 14d; GL, MS9171/7, f. 39; Oxley, Fletchers and Longbowstringmakers, p. 80.

form, beyond attendance at mass on St. John's day, the maintenance of the light, and an annual obit for the deceased, the Fletchers' devotions at the Austin Friars might have taken, but it is tempting to speculate whether at least individual members developed some connexion with the fraternity of St. Sebastian which had its home (and from 1496 an altar dedicated to the saint) in the friary.[101]

With the Reformation, the doctrine of Purgatory was abandoned, the individual's passage into heaven being now deemed to be dependent exclusively on the grace of God.[102] It is all the more interesting to see that a form of collective commemoration of the deceased continued. Even before the new religious ideas took over, individual fletchers had made provision for communal gatherings of the members of their livery in their memory. In 1537, Hugh Partriche assigned to the Fletchers' Company 13s. 4d. for a 'recreation among them of the clothing' after his burial;[103] six years later, John Wilshire, warden of the Company in 1521, 1529 and 1538, provided 20s. for a similar 'recreation' to be held by the present and former wardens

---

101 Little is known of this fraternity, but the cult of St. Sebastian was more common on the Continent than in England, and the fraternity at Austin Friars may also have been a gathering point for aliens. There was in addition a chantry dedicated to SS. Fabian and Sebastian in the hospital of St. Katherine by the Tower, founded by Edward III. Although in the middle ages chiefly venerated as a protector from the plague, in the light of his purported martyrdom by being shot with arrows St. Sebastian would have been a saint particularly appropriate to the Fletchers' craft. Holder, *Friaries of Medieval London*, pp. 132, 139–40; TNA, LR 15/13; E 159/240, *brevia directa* Trin. rot. 1; O. Gecser, 'Intercession and Specialization: St Sebastian and St Roche as Plague Saints and their Cult in Medieval Hungary', in *Les saints et leur culte en Europe centrale au Moyen Âge (xie-debut du xvie siècle)*, ed. M.-M. de Cevins and O. Marin, *Hagiologia*, xiii (2017), 77–108. St. Sebastian shared the manner of his martyrdom with a more widely venerated home-grown saint, St. Edmund of East Anglia. It is interesting to speculate whether the Fletchers' craft was deemed too lowly to associate itself with this 'royal' saint who was routinely depicted in royal pageantry, including pageants staged in the City of London on royal occasions: P. Webster, 'The Cult of St Edmund, King and Martyr, and the Medieval Kings of England', *History*, cv (2020), 636–51, and more generally F. Young, *Edmund: In Search of England's Lost King* (London and New York, 2018), ch. 4.

102 Like every company of the day, the Fletchers must have encompassed a variety of doctrinal beliefs and attitudes. In 1541 the fletchers John Starky and John Wilshire were among a number of early evangelicals from the parish of St. Magnus tried before the royal heresy commissioners for deviation from the Six Articles enshrined in statute in 1539, in their case for 'maintaining preachers of the new learning', such as Thomas Rose and Robert Wisdom, at the time among the most prominent evangelical preachers in London. The Austin friary, in whose church the Fletchers met for their communal devotions, had played a part in promoting the new thinking, and it is possible that this provided an avenue for it to spread among the members of the company. *The Acts and Monuments of John Foxe*, ed. S.R. Cattley (8 vols., London, 1838–41), v. 444; D.J. Wickman, 'The Religious Allegiance of London's Ruling Elite 1520–1603' (Univ. of London Ph.D. thesis, 1995), p. 113; R. Rex, 'The Friars in the English Reformation', in *The Beginnings of English Protestantism*, ed. P. Marshall and A. Ryrie (Cambridge, 2002), pp. 38–59, p. 40; A. Ryrie, *The Gospel and Henry VIII: Evangelicals in the Early English Reformation* (Cambridge, 2003), pp. 268–70.

103 GL, MS 9171/10, f. 299v.

at the Fletchers' Hall.[104] Some idea of the nature of these 'recreations' is provided by the will of John Romynge of High Holborn, who assigned to the Company four angel nobles 'to make them a dryncking'.[105]

These, ultimately secular gatherings continued unhindered even after the old practices and beliefs had been stripped away by the reformers, and the Fletchers clearly continued to value their 'recreations': in 1570, William Sherman bequeathed 20*s.* to 'the masters and lyverye of the companye' of Fletchers for a 'recreation' on the day of his burial, and five years later, John Martyn, a former warden, found a similar sum for such a gathering. In 1580 John Wardall (warden 1559, 1560, 1570, and 1579) left the Company 20*s.* 'for a repaste amongest them to be had in the daie of my buriall' and ten years later his widow, Joan, followed suit, assigning to the Fletchers 13*s.* 4*d.* 'to make them a bankett'.[106] There may now have been an added emphasis on the role of the members of the Company at the funeral itself. Martyn requested that the liverymen of his Company might accompany his body to his funeral; Sherman asked that four 'honeste Yonge menne' of the Company should bear his body to church; Joan Wardall made her bequest to the Fletchers contingent on their attendance at her burial, and in 1592 Thomas Butler left 20*s.* to the Fletchers' Company, 'to bringe my bodie to the earthe'.[107]

It was also Martyn whose will of 1576 provides the earliest evidence of the Fletchers' communal charitable activity in the modern sense. He assigned to the Company the sum of £6, to be made available annually in the form of loans of 20*s.* to up to three fellow fletchers who had fallen on hard times, the money being repayable by the end of the calendar year in which the loan had been made.[108]

Another consequence of the religious changes of the sixteenth century may have been an increased focus of the Company's communal gatherings on the Fletchers' Hall. The Company was in possession of a hall by 1518,[109] presumably the same tenement in the parish of St. Mary Axe referred to in 1535 in the royal accounts for the former property of the priory of Holy Trinity Aldgate (surrendered to the Crown in 1532) as 'Fletchers Hawle', for which the Company then paid an annual rent of 2*s.*[110] While it is possible that the Fletchers had availed themselves of the change of ownership when the last prior handed his house over to the King, the inclusion of the rent in early lists of the priory's possessions does suggest that the Company had previously been the priory's tenants, and had thus occupied the premises

---

104 GL, MS 9171/11, f. 95v.

105 TNA, PROB 11/30, f. 192r.

106 GL, MSS 9051/4, f. 195; 9171/17, f. 297v.

107 TNA, PROB 11/52, ff. 197v–198; PROB 11/58, ff. 59–59v; PROB 11/79, f. 293.

108 For the charitable activities of the livery companies after the Reformation more generally, see e.g. Rappaport, *Worlds within Worlds*, pp. 197–201.

109 LMA, Repertory 3, f. 261r.

110 *LP Hen. VIII*, xiii (2), no. 18.

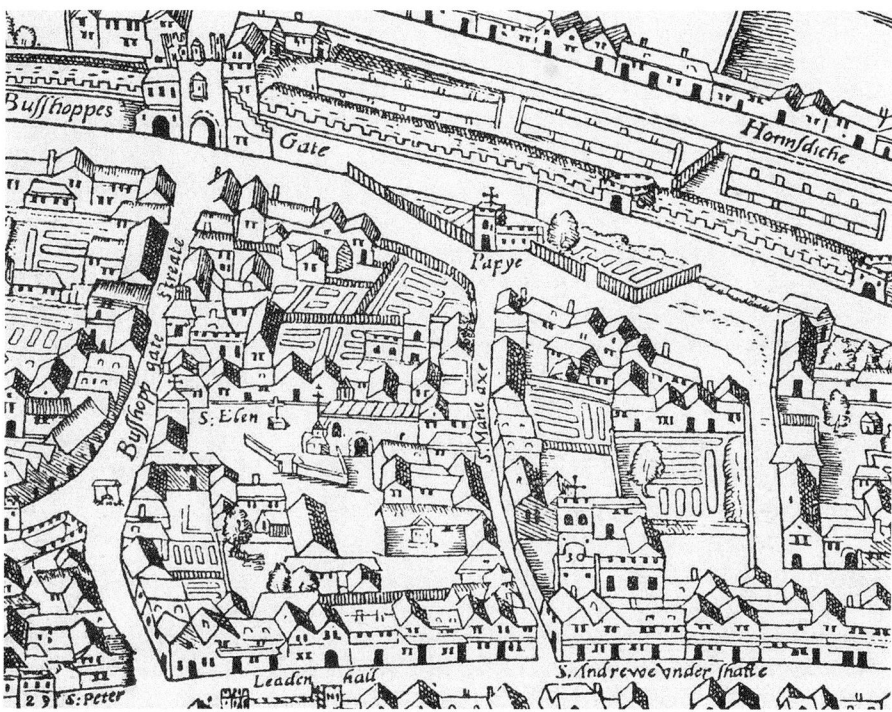

FIG. 5: Detail from the 'Agas' map of London c.1561, showing the area around
St. Mary Axe, with the Fletchers' Hall at the upper (north-eastern) end of the street.
© London Metropolitan Archives (City of London).

for some years before 1532.[111] The hall's location at the northern end of St.
Mary Axe was first recorded by the antiquarian John Stow in 1598, but Stow
offers no further details of the building's appearance. It has to be a matter
of speculation that it was in repairs to the hall that the Fletchers employed
the two altar stones that they bought from the churchwardens of St. Mary
Axe in 1550, when the church was stripped of such fixtures.[112] Only in
1720 did the ecclesiastical historian John Strype in his new and updated
edition of Stow's text describe the hall as 'a pretty small Brick Building' It
is impossible to be sure whether this was the original hall, but lying on the
outskirts of the City, the Fletchers' Hall had presumably survived the Great
Fire of 1666 unscathed.[113]

---

111 *LP Hen. VIII*, xiii (1), nos, 12, 48; TNA, SC 6/HENVIII/2356, 2363–2366; SC 12/11/16, f.
     7v.

112 TNA, E 117/4/65, m. 4.

113 John Strype, *A Survey of the Cities of London and Westminster* (2 vols., London, 1720), i. 82.
     Following reconstruction work in 1988 and again in 2007 the former site of the Fletchers'
     Hall is now practically unrecognisable: J. Milward, *46–50 St Mary Axe, London EC3A 8EL: Post-*

In all of the Company's collective activities, the visual expression of its corporate identity had an important part to play. On public occasions, members of the livery were expected to wear their gowns, and the regular renewal of these garments required by the Company's ordinances suggests that they were also donned on other occasions, perhaps the Fletchers' annual gathering at the Austin Friars, or the funerals and wakes of deceased members. Liverymen who refused to acquire new robes when the livery was renewed were subject to sanction. Such requirements served to set the liverymen apart from the lesser members of the Company, but it also expressed their identity as fletchers when they made their way through the streets of the City. The same applied when the Fletchers participated in public events alongside other companies, and these also provided occasions on which the Company's arms could be displayed. For a 'warrior company' the acquisition of armigerous status may have had added poignancy, but certainly it put the Fletchers as one of the lesser companies on a par with their greater neighbours: it may have been no accident that while four of the earliest known grants of arms to London companies went to guilds among the 'Great Twelve', three others went to companies much further down the hierarchy, the Cooks, Glovers and Upholders.[114]

An interesting, but ultimately unanswerable, question concerns the early Fletchers' Company's resources.[115] Under the terms of the Company's ordinances of 1484, every member was to pay a sum of 2d. at each of the four annual quarter days. In keeping with the Company's likely origins as a religious fraternity this money was explicitly assigned to the maintenance of the light of St. John in the Austin Friars. The Fletchers' only other formal source of communal income were the fines that the wardens could impose on rule breakers. These had to be shared with the City Chamber, and varied from year to year. Completely unpredictable were legacies from deceased members, which were in any event often assigned to a particular purpose such as a communal repast.

The Fletchers' earliest quarterage rolls seem to suggest that by the second decade of the sixteenth century members paid quarterage at two different rates of 2d. and 3d. per quarter respectively. It is not known when or why this change was introduced, but a possible factor could have been the need to find the annual rent for the Fletchers' Hall. As the original quarterage

Excavation Assessment Report (Wessex Archaeology, 2008). Available through the Archaeology Data Service (https://doi.org/10.5284/1027838).

114 Davies, 'Crown, City and Guild in Late Medieval London', pp. 263–4; Barron, *London in the Later Middle Ages*, p. 211; C.M. Barron, 'Chivalry, Pageantry and Merchant Culture in Medieval London', in *Heraldry, Pageantry and Social Display in Medieval England*, ed. P. Coss and M. Keen (Woodbridge, 2002), pp. 219–41, at pp. 239–41; Gadd, '"Ornamental for Closet or House"', pp. 55–6.

115 For an example of the finances of another impecunious company in the late fifteenth and early sixteenth centuries, see *The Pinners' and Wiresellers' Book, 1462–1511*, ed. B. Megson (London Record Society xliv, 2009).

was earmarked to pay for the light at Austin Friars, and income from fines and legacies was unpredictable, a further regular income stream had to be found to fund this new annual commitment, not to mention the costs of repairs to and the maintenance of the Company's premises. While the senior members of the Company invariably paid the higher rate, and new additions to its ranks were more likely to be assigned the lower one, the exact distinction between the two groups is unclear, and may have been based on economic circumstances, which were not invariably synonymous with an individual's status in the Fletchers' ranks.

After 1559, the quarterage rolls cease to record the two separate rates. If the payments originally associated with the cult of St. John had continued to be collected after their original purpose had fallen victim to religious change, they may perhaps have reverted to a single rate, all the income, rather than just any surplus, now going into Company coffers. Even so, the funds available to the Fletchers were never substantial, and it is likely that successive wardens had to work hard to find the money required to maintain the Company's place in City life.

The Fletchers in public life

The Fletchers might be one of the smaller and poorer companies of London, but this did not preclude them from playing their part in public life, even from the earliest years of the Company's existence. The years immediately following the separation of the Fletchers and Bowyers were marked in London by protracted political unrest, and a constitutional experiment that for a time sought to shift some political power to the companies: for a period of eight years between 1376 and 1384 the members of the City's Common Council were elected by the individual misteries, rather than on a geographical basis by wards, an arrangement which certainly benefited the smaller crafts, such as the newly independent Fletchers.[116] The fletchers John Bonet and Thomas Prentys were elected to the first of these councils in August 1376, and in 1381–2 the men so chosen were John Shordich and John Orchard, while other members of the craft were included in subsequent years.[117] One of the principal default lines between the London companies in these years was the division between the victualling and non-victualling trades, and it is thus not surprising to see the Fletchers on the side of the latter, when a number of London companies came to present petitions to the 'Merciless Parliament' of 1388, seeking the conviction of the former mayor Nicholas Brembre and the removal from office of his then serving successor, the fishmonger Nicholas Exton. At the same time, there may be an indication of the comparatively modest status of the Fletchers in these weighty matters in their decision to present a joint petition with the Bowyers, Cutlers, Spurriers and Bladesmiths, rather than going it alone, as the greater companies (but also the lowly Pinners) did.[118]

---

116 For a detailed discussion of these constitutional developments, see R. Bird, *The Turbulent London of Richard II* (London et al., 1948), esp. pp. 30–43, and *The London Jubilee Book, 1376–1387*, ed. C.M. Barron and L. Wright (London Record Society lv, 2021), pp. 1–18.

117 LMA, Letter Book H, f. 44; *Calendar of Plea and Memoranda Rolls of the City of London, 1381–1412*, ed. A.H. Thomas (London, 1932), p. 29; Bird, *Turbulent London*, pp. 122–31.

118 TNA, SC 8/21/1006.

With the end of the constitutional experiment in the mid 1380s, the influence of the smaller crafts once again waned in favour of the greater merchants, although individual fletchers naturally continued to play their part in the life of their parishes and wards. In the absence of eloquent records like early accounts of expenditure it is hard to draw any inferences as to the Fletchers' interaction and cooperation with other companies, other than perhaps the Bowyers. It is nevertheless interesting to speculate to what extent the Fletchers' ban on its members' attendance at fairs outside London owed something to an ongoing campaign by the leading men of the Mercers' Company to extend just such a ban to all freemen of London. It is possible that the wardens of the Fletchers regarded the ban (which was opposed even by the poorer members of the Mercers and which was just three years later superseded by an act of Parliament) as a measure designed to control the prices of their goods and (like the limitations on the amount of goods displayed for sale) to ensure fair competition.[119] Equally, while the Fletchers' ordinances leave little doubt that they shared their neighbours' dislike of outsiders and were sympathetic to any restrictions placed upon their access to London's commerce, it is impossible to know whether they actively collaborated with other companies in lobbying or petitioning King and Parliament for anti-alien, or indeed other legislation, as they had done in 1386.[120]

In other contexts, however, the Fletchers were far from invisible. In a culture that relied heavily on visual expressions of status and power, considerable significance was attached to the pageantry that accompanied important public events, and in this all the companies played their part. Whenever the King came to London it was customary for the citizens to ride out and greet him, before accompanying him through the streets where pageants would be staged. This was, for instance, the case when Henry V paid his last living visit to the City in February 1422, when the citizens rode out in white gowns with red hoods; in 1463 when there were six Fletchers among the citizens who rode out to meet Edward IV; and in 1483 when the young Edward V arrived in London. Perhaps on account of the cost to the City of providing the uniform robes worn by the representatives of the companies on these occasions, numbers began to be scaled back, and only two fletchers participated on the occasions of the arrivals of Richard III after crushing Buckingham's rebellion in the autumn

---

119 A.F. Sutton, *The Mercery of London: Trade, Goods and People, 1130–1578* (Aldershot, 2005), pp. 214–16; *Parliament Rolls*, ed. Given Wilson et al., xv. 377–8.

120 For the lobbying of Parliament by London companies, including some of the artisans like the Carpenters and Pewterers, see M.P. Davies, 'Lobbying Parliament: The London Companies in the Fifteenth Century', in *Parchment and People. Parliament in the Middle Ages*, ed. L.S. Clark, *Parliamentary History*, xxiii (2004), 136–48. For the anti-alien legislation of 1484 and the lobbying that led up to it, see A.F. Sutton and L. Visser-Fuchs, *Richard III's Books* (Stroud, 1997), pp. 244–50.

of 1483, and Henry VII after the battles of Bosworth in 1485 and Stoke in 1487.[121]

On the occasion of a royal coronation, it was likewise customary for the new monarch (or queen consort) to spend the night in the Tower of London, before riding through the City to Westminster abbey for the ceremony. The streets of London would be lined by the citizens, their turnout marshalled and organised by the companies. When Edward IV's queen, Elizabeth Wydeville, rode to the Tower in 1465 six fletchers formed part of the official lineup, and it is probable that a similar delegation had played its part four years earlier when Edward himself was crowned in the summer of 1461.[122] In 1509, when the young Henry VIII and his queen, Katherine of Aragon, rode through the City it was provided by the Court of Aldermen that each company should provide rails behind which its members would stand, their length presumably determined as much by the size of the membership, as by the company's finances. The greater companies paraded in Cheapside, while further down the social hierarchy, the Fletchers found themselves closer to the Tower, a considerable distance from the Mercers at the head of the line-up. There were also more sombre occasions, such as royal funerals at Westminster. In the autumn of 1422, when Henry V's body arrived from France the mayor, aldermen and greater citizens, clad in black, met the funeral procession at St. George's Bar in Southwark, and conducted the carriage bearing the King's coffin over the Bridge into the City. They were accompanied by 300 representatives of the crafts dressed in white and bearing torches, of which the Fletchers and Bowyers between them provided six.[123]

Royal entries aside, London's civic year was also punctuated by a number of festivities and ceremonials in which the companies participated. Among these were the annual midsummer watches held on the nights of the feast days of the Nativity of St. John the Baptist (24 June) and St. Peter and St. Paul (29 June).[124] Such watches had been held in London by the early thirteenth century, but the associated ceremonial and pageantry had been much enhanced in the later fourteenth century, and a mobile watch that marched through the City had been introduced in addition to the watches mounted in each ward. In the course of the fifteenth century, further pageantry, images of giants, and Morris dancers were added to the spectacle, and in the early sixteenth century, the Court of Aldermen laid down the numbers of 'bowmen' that each company was to provide to the procession. While the greatest companies each provided eight watchmen,

---

121 Oxley, *Fletchers and Longbowstringmakers*, pp. 89–90.
122 *Ibid.*
123 LMA, Letter Book K, f. 1v.
124 For these watches see S. Lindenbaum, 'Ceremony and Oligarchy: the London Midsummer Watch' in *City and Spectacle in Medieval Europe*, ed. B. Hanawalt and K.L. Ryerson (Minneapolis, 1994), pp. 171–88.

the Fletchers, like the Bowyers, Butchers, Ironmongers, Armourers, and some other others, every year found four men.[125]

It is likely that the Fletchers' contribution to the midsummer watches resembled that at the annual Mayor's Riding (the precursor of the modern Lord Mayor's Show) that evolved at about the same time. By the fifteenth century the elected mayor's annual trip to Westminster on 28 October to take his oath to the King had become the occasion for elaborate pageantry. The mayor was accompanied by representatives of the companies dressed in their livery robes, and by the end of the 1470s the associated spectacle had become so overwhelming that in 1481 the authorities laid down that 'there shall no disguysyng nor pageoun be used or hadde ... like as it hath been used nowe of late'.[126]

If such pageants may ultimately have been to those participating a source of enjoyment or at least satisfaction, as much out of justifiable pride in their company, and in their City, the companies were also subject to more onerous duties and charges. A long-standing concern of the London authorities was the obstruction of traffic on the river Thames by fish weirs and the connected threat posed to the river's fish stocks by the illegal use of fine nets that would catch very young fish before they had spawned. Attempts by the Londoners to restore order and to destroy such illegal weirs and obstructions met with resistance by their owners, and the Crown repeatedly proved reluctant to become directly involved, In the late spring of 1421 Parliament ordered that the mayor of London should henceforth carry out quarterly inspections of the watercourse and remove any irregular obstructions and weirs. As had previously happened in 1406, the mayor sought the assistance of the livery companies to overcome the expected opposition. Each company's contribution depended on its size and wealth, and the Fletchers were instructed to man a barge jointly with the Girdlers, Salters, Barbers, Brewers, Dyers and Tallowchandlers. Yet, the Fletchers refused, arguing that they could not spare the manpower, as they were too busy manufacturing arrows for the King. This was not a point with which the City fathers could argue: news of the English defeat at the battle of Baugé and the death of the King's brother, Thomas, duke of Clarence, had caused Henry V to cut short his progress through his kingdom, and to speed up preparations for his return to France at the head of an army (including more than 3,000 archers), and – even if some of the required armaments were procured elsewhere in the kingdom – there can be little doubt that London's fletchers were working overtime to produce the arrows needed. The mayor therefore agreed that the Fletchers would not have to attend

---

125 Barron, 'Chivalry, Pageantry and Merchant Culture', pp. 228–9; LMA, Journal 11, f. 347v; Journal 12, f. 334v; Letter Book O, f. 243v (all printed in *Records of Early English Drama: Civic London to 1558*, ed. A. Lancashire (Woodbridge, 2015), pp. 345, 431, 497).

126 Barron, 'Chivalry, Pageantry and Merchant Culture', 229. Quotation from *Calendar of Letter-Books of the City of London: L, Edward IV–Henry VII*, ed. R.R. Sharpe (London, 1912), p. 187.

in their own persons, but should pay towards the cost of the enterprise like other companies – in itself no trifling matter: the Brewers' contribution to the same expedition cost that company as much as £2 2s.[127]

From the 1520s it was common practice for the mayor and aldermen to raise loans from the companies to pay for the maintenance of a communal store of grain to tide the City over in times of scarcity, and from the 1540s such loans were demanded nearly every year. The Fletchers, in keeping with their modest wealth, contributed a rather smaller sum than the greater companies, but the £15 they found in 1546 still represented a substantial outlay, even if it amounted to a mere fraction of the £150 a piece lent by the Grocers, Drapers, Mercers or Merchant Taylors. It was nevertheless an important gesture, since it did cement the Fletchers' claim to be counted among the 'cheyf companyes' of the City.[128]

---

127 GL, MS 5440, ff. 56v–57r. I am grateful to Mrs. Caroline Metcalfe for this document. C.M. Barron, 'The Government of London and its Relations with the Crown 1400–1450' (Univ. of London Ph.D. thesis, 1970), esp. pp. 357–8; J. Doig, 'Propaganda and Truth: Henry V's Royal Progress in 1421', *Nottingham Mediaeval Studies*, xl (1998), 167–79, p. 170; J.H. Wylie and W.T. Waugh, *The Reign of Henry the Fifth* (3 vols., Cambridge, 1914–29), iii. 317–19.

128 Unwin, Gilds and Companies of London, p. 239; LMA, Repertory 11, ff. 266r–v. The Bowyers' and Armourers' Companies, like the Fletchers, contributed £15. In all, 28 companies contributed in 1546.

The end of the 'first phase'

The evolution of gunpowder weaponry is central to the story of the development of military technology in the later middle ages, and it ultimately also brought about the decline of the fletchers' craft and trade. As the crossbow and longbow were increasingly superseded by firearms, the demand for the thousands of arrows that had previously been manufactured melted away. In the first instance, some of the decline was stayed by an insistence on the part of the authorities that recreational archery be maintained both as an essential defensive skill, and as a wholesome alternative to games and leisure pursuits, such as tennis, bowls, or later 'slydethrifte otherwise called shovegrote', deemed morally subversive. In 1512 an act of Parliament (reaffirmed three years later) required all able-bodied laymen between the ages of seventeen and sixty to keep a bow and arrows, and to undertake regular archery practice. Boys between the ages of seven and seventeen were to be taught to shoot by their fathers or guardians, and were to be given a bow and two arrows with which to practice.[129] From 1504, the ownership of first crossbows, and subsequently also handguns, was by law restricted to those who could meet a minimum income qualification, or who could show urgent need for their possession for the defence of the realm or of their property.[130] A statute of 1542 painted a bleak picture of the state of the crafts making bows and arrows in the City of London. The lack of demand for such weaponry, it was suggested, had caused many bowyers and fletchers to seek work outside the realm of England, thus taking and teaching their ancient expertise to foreigners. Moreover, the Londoners' longstanding concern over workmen from elsewhere in England setting up unregulated shops in London's suburbs once more came to the fore, not

---

129 *Statutes of the Realm* (11 vols, London, 1810–28, repr. 1963), iii. 25–6, 123–4 (3 Hen. VIII, c. 3, 13; 6 Hen. VIII, c. 2); Oxley, *Fletchers and Longbowstringmakers*, p. 29.
130 *Statutes of the Realm*, iii. 32–3, 132–3, 215–16, 457–9, 832–5 (3 Hen. VIII, c. 13; 6 Hen. VIII, c. 13; 14–15 Hen. VIII, c. 7; 25 Hen. VIII, c. 17; 33 Hen. VIII, c. 6).

only depriving London-trained artisans of work, but also denuding other parts of England of competent bowyers and fletchers.[131]

If this legislation, as was not uncommon, painted an excessively negative picture of the state of archery in early sixteenth-century England, it may have been to some extent effective in providing a remedy. Recent research has suggested that while the pursuit of archery faltered in parallel with its importance in warfare in the 1520s and 30s, as a recreational practice at least it saw something of a resurgence from the 1540s, and did not again enter a downward spiral until the reign of Elizabeth I.[132] Elements beyond the commercial viability of the trade may also have played a part in the Company's temporary decline in the mid sixteenth century. In the light of the centrality of religious ceremonies and intercessory prayer in the Fletchers' early communal life, it is hard not to suspect a connexion between the decline of the membership in the 1530s and the religious upheavals of these years. The numbers of members named on the quarterage rolls of the London Fletchers' Company lend support such a view. Having hovered around 95 in the 1520s, it was the decade from 1529 to 1538 that saw the membership drop to as low as 67 in 1535.

From the 1540s, however, the membership of the Company began to recover and grow once more. In 1560 the Fletchers numbered over 100, and there were more than 130 of them in 1572. Yet, this was not a recovery that was unequivocally brought about by a renewed demand for the fletchers' wares, and by the early 1570s the leading men of the London Company were growing worried about the economic fortunes of its younger members. In 1572 it was thus decided to restrict the number of apprentices any master might keep at any one time. In spite of this measure, the membership of the Company continued to outgrow the declining demand for arrows, and just two decades later, in 1592, the Fletchers found it necessary to further restrict the progress of young members of the craft into the ranks of the independent owners of workshops. Men admitted to the freedom of the Company were now required to serve a term of two years as journeymen before they could set themselves up independently, and were barred from taking apprentices in the first year of their independence. Interestingly, these terms approved by the mayor and aldermen halved the periods of restriction of four and two years respectively for which the Fletchers had originally asked.[133]

In common with other London companies, the Fletchers redefined their activities in the wake of the Reformation, and a resurgence of recreational archery gave them a continued *raison d'être* as a craft organisation. Yet, what

---

131 *Statutes of the Realm*, iii. 837–8 (33 Hen. VIII, c. 9); Davies, 'Aliens, crafts and guilds', pp. 136–37.

132 S. Gunn, 'Archery Practice in Early Tudor England', *Past and Present*, ccix (2010), 53–81, *passim*.

133 LMA, Repertory 22, ff. 439v–440v. See appendix, no. 8.

allowed the Company its Indian summer in the second half of the sixteenth century was another factor: the Fletchers' status as one of the ancient livery companies of London. Membership of the Company offered a route to the freedom of the City, but it also conveyed wider privileges. The powers of social control and oversight vested in the wardens of any one of London's companies meant that complaints against any of their members would in the first instance be adjudicated by the leading men of the individual's company.[134] In terms of such jurisdiction over their membership, the Fletchers were the equals of any of the greater companies, even if these could expect to exercise authority at the higher levels of the civic hierarchy from which their lesser neighbours, like the Fletchers, remained largely excluded. Increasingly, membership of the Fletchers' Company, like that of other historic companies whose original activities had been partly or completely superseded by technological advances, was thus sought by men with no stake in the fletchers' traditional craft. That this was so is suggested by the appearance in the Company's quarterage lists in the last quarter of the sixteenth century of men described by different trades or crafts altogether, such as Anthony Barrowe (*d.*1596), 'knifemaker', Henry Noskyn (*d.*1602), shoemaker, and William Alder (*d.*1594), draper. The style of 'citizen and fletcher' was increasingly becoming an honorific, rather than a designation of trade.[135]

In economic terms, the Fletchers had never been able to compete with the great merchant companies like the Mercers, Drapers or Grocers, but its liverymen nevertheless played a privileged part in the City's life. During the second century of their independent existence, their craft might have gradually declined as a commercial concern, but as a company the Fletchers nevertheless continued to flourish during and beyond what has been described as the 'golden age of the livery companies'.[136]

---

134 Rappaport, *Worlds within Worlds*, p. 213.
135 GL, MS 5977/2, mm. 15–24.
136 Rappaport, *Worlds within Worlds*, p. 213.

Known Wardens of the Fletchers' Company, 1385–1603

Date	Wardens	Source
1385–86	Nicholas Bonet	William Jerberge	LMA, Letter Book H, f. 195v
1386–87	Stephen Seder	Robert atte Verne	LMA, Letter Book H, f. 206
1387–88	William Aystone	Nicholas Minot	LMA, Letter Book H, f. 222v
1418–19	John Loveyn	John Turnour	LMA, Letter Book I, f. 221
1420–21	John Hall	Richard Otehill	LMA, Letter Book I, f. 249
1424–25	Roger Daveney	Walter Takeneswell	LMA, Letter Book K, f. 30v
1428–29	William Crane	John Turnour	LMA, Letter Book K, f. 65v
1431–32	Thomas Scott	Richard Otehill	LMA, Letter Book K, f. 106v
1432–33	John Parker	Thomas Scot	LMA, Letter Book K, f. 114v
1438–39	Henry Hoggys	John Large	LMA, Letter Book K, f. 173
1441–42	John Hammond	John Frampton	LMA, Letter Book K, f. 195
1460–61	Henry Crane	Henry Felde	TNA, E 159/238, *brevia directa* Hil. rot. 14d
1488–90	Robert Holmenby (Holdynby)	Richard Baxster	LMA, Jnl. 9, ff. 288x, 293
1490–92	Simon Motte	John Burdon	LMA, Jnl. 9, ff. 273, 280
1519–20	Christopher Pynkeney	William Smyth	GL, MS 5977/1, m. 1
1521–23	John Wilshire	Thomas Higson	GL, MS 5977/1, m. 2

Date	Wardens		Source
1525–27	Thomas Cony	Richard Rutland	GL, MS 5977/1, m. 3
1527–29	William Temple	Lewis Owen	GL, MS 5977/1, m. 4
1529–31	John Wilshire	Thomas Higson	GL, MS 5977/1, m. 5
1535–36	William Smyth	John Fremynger	GL, MS 5977/1, m. 6
1536–37	Thomas Higson	Robert Michell	GL, MS 5977/1, m. 7
1537–38	William Sherman	Robert Hughson	GL, MS 5977/1, m. 8
1538–39	John Wilshire	Thomas Smyth	GL, MS 5977/1, m. 9
1542–44	Thomas Nele	Nicholas Bageley	GL, MS 5977/1, m. 10
1544–45	William Smyth	John Hervy	GL, MS 5977/1, m. 11
1545–46	William Sherman	William Northey	GL, MS 5977/1, m. 12
1559–60	William Sherman	John Wardall	GL, MS 5977/2, m. 1
1560–61	William Sherman	John Wardall	GL, MS 5977/2, m. 2
1566–67	William Longe	Thomas Deane	GL, MS 5977/2, m. 3
1568–69	Thomas Crompe	John Smyth	GL, MS 5977/2, m. 4
1570–71	John Wardall	Robert Kirbye	GL, MS 5977/2, m. 5
1571–72	John Hodgettes	John Martyn	GL, MS 5977/2, m. 6

Date	Wardens		Source
1572–73	John Philippes	John Cockes	GL, MS 5977/2, m. 7
1573–74	Richard Bletcher	John Kylby	GL, MS 5977/2, m. 8
1574–75	William Longe	Robert Broughe	GL, MS 5977/2, m. 9
1575–76	Thomas Crompe	David Powell	GL, MS 5977/2, m. 10
1577–78	John Smyth	John Thompson	GL, MS 5977/2, m. 11
1579–80	John Wardall	John Johnson	GL, MS 5977/2, m. 12
1580–81	John Cockes	John Hayes	GL, MS 5977/2, m. 13
1582–83	Robert Broughe	Roger Snowdon	GL, MS 5977/2, m. 14
1583–84	David Powell	John Howle	GL, MS 5977/2, m. 15
1585–86	John Thompson	John Haywarde	GL, MS 5977/2, m. 17
1587–88	Thomas Dowsing	John Haywarde	GL, MS 5977/2, m. 18
1588–89	John Johnson	William Reynold	GL, MS 5977/2, m. 19
1590–91	Peter Michell	Humphrey Daly	GL, MS 5977/2, m. 20
1594–95	John Howle	Edmund Rolf	GL, MS 5977/2, m. 16
1598–99	Robert Kirbye	Edmund Fayrfax	GL, MS 5977/2, m. 22
1600–01	Robert Broughe	William Osborne	GL, MS 5977/2, m. 23
1602–03	David Powell	Edward Sicklyng	GL, MS 5977/2, m. 24

The Early Ordinances of the Fletchers of London, c.1371–1592[137]

1. Petition of the good men of the crafts of Bowyers and Fletchers of London to the mayor and aldermen of London, seeking judgment and sanction on four individuals who have refused to abide by the agreement of the two crafts that no one man shall practice both. 7 March 1371. (LMA, City of London Letter Book G, f. 266v)

Die Veneris in festo sanctarum Perpetue et Felicitatis anno regni regis Edwardi tercij post conquestum quadragesimo quinto venerunt hic probi homines de mestero de Bowyers London' [et] liberaverunt maiori et aldermannis quandam billam in hec verba:

[here follows the Bowyers' prohibition of night-time working]

Et similiter predicti probi homines de mistero predicto et alij probi homines de mestero de Fleccers London' liberaverunt maiori, Recordatori et aldermannis predictis quandam aliam billam in hec verba:

As honurables et sages seignurs, mair, Recordour et audermans de la cite de Loundres monstrent les bones gentz par vn assent et a corde del

---

137 In the following texts common abbreviations have been silently expanded, and a degree of punctuation introduced. Editorial interventions are indicated by square brackets.

mestiers de Bowyers et Flecchers de Loundres qe com il est ordeyne et a
corde finablement entre les ditz gentz dune mestier et dautre pur profit et
auantage de toute la commune qe nul homme de lun mestier mellera od
lautre mestier en nul point as queux couenantz tenir fermez et establez a
parfourmr[138] touz les gentz des auantditz mestier sont acordez horspris qatre
hommes par nouns Johan Patyn, Robert atte Verne, Richard Prodhomme
et Johan Lyon qi ne voillent as ditz ordinances assenter. Si suppliant touz
les bonez gentz des auantdites mestiers qe plese a vostre droiturel seignurie
faire venir les dites qatre hommes nomez pardeuant vous a les Justifier par
lauantdite ordinance en auantage et commune profit com dit est deuant. Et
ke si nul homme del vn mester[139] \se/ melle en lautre mester en nul point
apres ses heures qil paie a la Chambre de la Gyhall a la premer defaute xls.
et a la secunde defaute iiij li. Et issint a chescun defaute le double com les
auantditz bones gentz entre eaux ount ordeyne.

Postea venerunt predicti Johannes Patyn, Robertus atte Verne, Ricardus
Prodhomme et Johannes Lyon coram eosdem Maiore et aldermannis et
concesserunt obseruare ordinacionem predictam et facere iuxta eandem
sicut superius ordinatum est etc. Et super hoc habito auisamento inter
maiorem et aldermannis super premissis etc. concordatum est et concessum
per eosdem quod articuli predicti in predictis duabus billis contenti de cetero
obseruentur sub penis supradictis pro communi proficio tocius populi etc.
Postea ad Husteng' de communibus placitis tentum die Lune proximo ante
festum sancti Gregorij pape anno regni regis Edwardi tercij post conquestum
xlv[to] veniunt predicti Johannes Patyn, Robertus atte Verne, Ricardus
Prodhomme et Johannes Lyon coram predictis Maiore et aldermannis et
dicunt quod ipsi habent diversas res de vtroque mestero predicto inceptas
ad operandum et quidam eorum \habent/ apprenticios vtriusque mesteri
et plures arcus et sagittas perfectas ad vendendum et petunt respectum
et licenciam predictas res de vtroque mestero predicto imperfectas
perficiendas et eas simul cum alijs arcubus et sagittis quas habent modo
perfectis vendicioni exponendas ab huic vsque ad festum Pasche proximo
futurum. Ita quod ipsi interim providere[140] possint ad quod predictorum
duorum mesterorum ipsi tunc se tenere velint, vnum mesterum inde ex
tunc \solummodo/ tenendum et excercendum in forma in predictis billis
contenta. Et concessum est eis etc. Inhibitum est eciam eis quod ipsi post
predictum festum Pasche non exercent nisi vnicum[141] mesterum de duobus
mesteris predictis quod eligere voluerint sub pena in predictis billis contenta
etc. Postea, videlicet die Lune proximo post festum sancti Laurencij anno xlv[to]
supradicto, veniunt hic probi homines de mistero de Bowyers et queruntur

---

138 *Sic.*
139 *Sic.*
140 MS 'interim v providere'.
141 MS 'unnicum'.

quod predictus Robertus atte Verne post predictum festum Pasche excercuit vtrumque misterum, videlicet tam de Bowyers quam de Flecchers, contra ordinacionem predictam etc., qui quidem Robertus die Martis proximo sequenti venit hic et non potuit hoc dedicere et inde posuit se in graciam maioris etc. Et coram ipso maiore et Recordatore ac hominibus de utrique mistero predicto tunc elegit et pecijt se admitti ad misterum de Bowyers de cetero solomodo excercendum. Et omnino renunciauit misterum de Flecchers. Et concessum est ei et preceptum similiter quod ipse de cetero non excerceat misterum de Flecchers sub pena supradicta etc.

Translation:
On Friday, the feast of SS Perpetua and Felicitas in the forty-fifth year of the reign of King Edward III after the Conquest, came here the good men of the craft of the bowyers of London and delivered to the mayor and aldermen a certain bill in these words:

[*here follows the Bowyers' prohibition of night-time working*]

And likewise the aforesaid good men of the aforesaid craft and other good men of the craft of the fletchers of London delivered to the aforesaid mayor, recorder and aldermen another bill in these words:

To the honourable and wise lords, the mayor, recorder and aldermen of the city of London, the good folk of the crafts of the bowyers and fletchers of London, by one assent and accord, show that whereas it has been ordained and finally agreed between the said folk of the one craft and of the other, for the profit and advantage of the entire community that no man of the one craft shall meddle with the other craft in any way, which covenants all the people of the aforesaid craft have agreed to firmly keep and act upon, except for four men by the names of John Patyn, Robert atte Verne, Richard Prodhomme and John Lyon, who will not agree to the said ordinances. So all the good folk of the aforesaid crafts pray that it may please your just masterships to cause the said four men named above to come before you to be judged according to the aforesaid ordinance to the advantage and common profit as is aforesaid. And so that no man of the one craft shall in any way meddle in the other craft after this hour, he shall pay to the Chamber of the Guildhall for the first infraction 40*s.*, and for the second infraction £4. And thus for every infraction double, as the aforesaid good folk have ordained between them.

Afterwards the aforesaid John Patyn, Robert atte Verne, Richard Prodhomme et John Lyon came before the same mayor and aldermen and agreed to observe the aforesaid ordinance and to do accordingly, as is ordained above etc. And over this, the mayor and aldermen having considered the premises etc., it was agreed and granted by the same that the aforesaid articles contained in the aforesaid two bills should henceforth be observed under the abovesaid penalties for the common profit of all the people etc. Afterwards at the Husting of common pleas held on Monday next after the feast of St Gregory the Pope in the forty-fifth year of the reign of King Edward III after the Conquest the aforesaid John Patyn, Robert atte Verne, Richard Prodhomme and John Lyon come before the aforesaid mayor and aldermen and say that they have begun to work various things of either aforesaid craft, and certain of them have apprentices of either craft and many completed bows and arrows to sell, and they ask for respite and licence from this day until the feast of Easter next to complete the aforesaid incomplete things of either craft, and to put them up for sale together with the other completed bows and arrows which they now have. So that in the mean time they may decide to which of the aforesaid two crafts they then want to keep themselves, keeping and exercising only one craft thereof in the form contained in the aforesaid bills. And this is conceded to them etc. They are also forbidden to exercise after the aforesaid feast of Easter more than one of the two aforesaid crafts, which they wish to select, under the penalty contained in the aforesaid bills etc. Afterwards, that is to say on Monday next after the feast of St Lawrence in the abovesaid forty-fifth year, the good men of the Bowyers' craft came here and complained that the aforesaid Robert atte Verne after the aforesaid feast of Easter exercised both crafts, that is to say both that of bowyers and that of fletchers contrary to the abovesaid ordinance etc., which Robert came here on the Tuesday then next following and could not deny this, and placed himself at the mayor's grace etc. And before the same mayor and recorder and the men of either craft he then chose and asked to be admitted henceforth to exercise only the craft of the bowyers. And he completely renounced the craft of the fletchers. And this is granted to him, and he is similarly commanded that he should henceforth not exercise the craft of fletchers under the abovesaid penalty etc.

2. Ordinance of the Fletchers' craft, providing for the annual election of the craft's wardens and their powers of search. 16 June 1403 (LMA, City of London Letter Book I, f. 24v)

Ordinacio mistere de Flecchers

Ordinacio mistere de Flecchers facta per Johannem Walcote, maiorem Ciuitatis London' et Aldermannos sextodecimo die Junij anno regni Regis Henrici quarti post conquestum quarto et que proclamata fuit vicesimo die Junij anno predicto etc.
Primerment qe les ditz gentz du dit mestier du dicte Citee eient poair chescun an a le feste de Seint Edward le Roy pour eslier deux personnes pur estre gardeins de mesme le mestier pur surveier et en serchier lan proschein

ensuiaunt toutz maners settes [glossed in a different ink: arowes] et testes de settes quarelles sibien des citezeins come foreins deins la dicte Citee et qils eient poair tiel artillarie troue faux et deceiuable arrestier sibien en maisons et la roiale chemyn come en chescun autre lieu deinz la fraunchise de la dicte Citee et les presenter as Mair et Aldermans qi pur le temps serront pur illeoqes estre.

Translation:
Ordinance of the fletchers' craft made by John Walcote, mayor of the city of London and the aldermen on 16 June in the fourth year of the reign of King Henry IV after the Conquest and which was proclaimed on 20 June in the aforesaid year etc.

Firstly, that the said folk of the said craft if the said city shall have power every year on the feast of St Edward the King to choose two persons to be wardens of the same craft to survey and search for the year then next following all manner of arrows and arrowheads and crossbow bolts both of citizens and foreigners in the said city, and they shall have power to seize such artillery found false and deceitful, both in houses and the King's highway, and in every other place within the liberty of the said city, and to present them to the mayor and aldermen for the time being.

3. Ordinance of the Fletchers' craft, prohibiting the opening of fletchers' shops on Sundays and major feast days. 8 May 1423. (LMA, City of London Letter Book K, f. 6).

Ordinacio mistere Flechars

Octauo die Maij Anno regni Regis Henrici sexti post conquestum primo venerunt hic coram Willelmo Walderne, Maiore, et Aldermannis in Camera Guyhalde Ciuitatis London' Magistri et probi homines Mistere de Flecchers dicte ciuitatis et porrexerunt eisdem Maiori et Aldermannis quondam billam siue peticionem verba subsequencia continentem:

As honurables et graciouses seignurs les Mair et Audermans de la Cite de Loundres Monstrent humblement les Gardeins et bones gentz de la Mistier de Flecchers de Loundres qe come diuerses persones de mesme la mistier teignent lour Shopes oeuertz les dismenges et aultres iours festiualx dont les veigles sount Jemynez et vendent settes et flecches et aultres diuerses choses et oeueraignes au dit Mistier appurtenantz et ensy ne gardent lour iour festiual a graund displesance et encounter la volunte de dieu et a graund perill de lour almes. Si please a voz honurables et graciouses seignuries de grauntier qe larticle vnsuant poet estre entre de record en la Chambre de la Guyhall come aultres ordeignances touchantz la bone reule et gouernance du dicte Mistier auoient estez adeuant et ceo principalment pur le plesir et honure de dieux pur dieux et en oeuere de charite. Cestassauoir qe null home du dicte Mistier deins a Fraunchise de la Cite suisdicte ne teigne sa Shope oeuert les dismenges ne null aultre iour festiual dont la veigle est jemynee pur vendre settes ne flecches nautres choses ne oeueraignes au dicte Mistier en ascun manere appurtenauntz sur peine de paier a chescun temps qil soit ent conuict vjs. viijd. lun moite al oeps de la Chambre de la Guyhall et lautre moite al oeps de la mistier suisdicte.

Qua quidem billa lecta et audita concessum et ordinatum est per dictos maiorem et aldermannos quod billa predicta iuxta tenorem et effectum eiusdem in omnibus decetero obseruetur et execucioni debite mancipetur quamdiu visu fuerit eisdem Maiori et Aldermannis Ciuitatis London' pro tempore existentibus ordinacionem huiusmodi fore bonam honestam et necessariam ac communi populo comodiferam etc.

Translation:
Ordinance of the Fletchers' Craft

The eighth day of May in the first year of the reign of King Henry VI after the Conquest came here before William Walderne, mayor, and the aldermen in the chamber of the guildhall of the city of London and masters and good men of the craft of fletchers of the said city and placed before the same mayor and aldermen a certain bill or petition, containing the following words:

To the honourable and gracious masters, the mayor and aldermen of the city of London, the wardens and good folk of the craft of fletchers of London show humbly that whereas various persons of the same craft keep their shops open on Sundays and other feast days with double vigils, and sell arrows and fleches and various other things and pieces of work pertaining to the said craft, and thus do not keep their feast day, to the great displeasure and contrary to the will of God and to the great peril of their souls. May it please your honourable and gracious masterships to grant that the following article may be entered of record in the Chamber of the Guildhall, as other ordinances touching the good rule and governance of the said craft have been in the past, and this principally for the pleasure and honour of God, for God and by work of charity. That is to say that no man of the said craft shall within the liberty of the said city keep his shop open on Sundays, nor on any other feast day with a double vigil to sell arrows nor fleches nor other things or pieces of work pertaining to the said craft in any way, under the penalty of paying for each time that they are convicted thereof 6*s.* 8*d.*, half to the use of the Chamber of the Guildhall and the other half to the use of the abovesaid craft.

Which bill having been read and heard, it was granted and ordained by the said mayor and aldermen that the aforesaid bill shall henceforth be observed in all things according to its tenor and effect, and put to due execution for as long as it shall appear to the same mayor and aldermen of the city of London for the time being that such an ordinance is good honest and necessary and beneficial to the common people etc.

4. Ordinance of the Fletchers' craft, prohibiting night-time working, and working in obscure places. 5 June 1432. (LMA, City of London Letter Book K, f. 106v).

Fait a remembrer qe le quint Jour de Juyn Lan du Regne le Roy Henry sisme puis le conquest disme venoient ycy deuant Johan Welles, Mair, et Audermans en la Graund Chambre du Guyhalle de la Cite de Loundres les bones gentz del Mistier de Flecchers de mesme la Cite et exhiberont as ditz Mair et Audermans vne bille contenantz deux Articles touchauntz le bon reugle et gouuernance de leur dit Mistier humblement suppliauntz de les suruerier et examiner et sur ceo les confermer e approuer taunt pour lonestice du dit Mistier come pur le bien et profit nostre seinur le Roy et son people, le teneur du quele bille censuyt et est tiel:

Monstrent Richard Otehill et Thomas Scot, Gardeins, et toutz les bones gentz enfraunchisez el[142] Mistier des Flecchers deins la Cite de Loundres qe come les seruantz et ouereurs de mesme la Mistier qi sount alowez pur faire bien et loialment settes et aultre manier dartelrie pur le bien du Roy et son people et en defence du Roialme de bone estuffe et secche merisme quele leur est deliuere par les ditz suppliauntz, souuentz foitz taunt dedeins la liberte du mesme la Cite come dehors dedeins leur chambres et aultres muscettes et places privez oueront noetaundre et chaungent ycell bone estuffe et secche merisme en vert merisme et aultre faux estuffe qi ne poet bien endure ne loialment deseruier a Roy ne son people et ent facent tielx settes et aultre manere dartelrie non soulement au graunt damage et dishonure des ditz supplianz, mais a greuouse destruccion du people du Roy. Si please a voz bons seigneuries de graunter et ordeigner qe les deux articles ensuantz qe sount de la commune assent de tout Mestier auantdit purueux encountre les mischiefs desuisdictes soient entrez de record icy deuaunt vous en la court nostre seignur le Roy et adiuggez par voz sages discrecions destre gardez et obseruez pur toutz Jours en temps auenir pur dieu et en oeure de charite.

En primes qe null homme Frank de mesme la Mistier desore enauant alowe ne mette dedeins la Fraunchise de Loundres ne dehors null oeuereur ne seruant du dit Mistier pur oeuerer ne faire ascun settes sinon en la propre

---

142 *Sic.*

maison ou il qi allowe ou mette tielx seruantz a oeuerer demurra au fin et entent qe dhue serche suruieu et correccion poet ester fait taunt sur tout tiel oeuere come lestuff dicelle qils soient bones et ables au profit du Roy et son people[143] sur peine de paier a chescun foitz qil serra conuict du contraire vjs. viijd. lun moite al oeps del Chambre de Guyhall suisdicte et lautre moite au dit Mistier.

Item qe null homme du mesme la Mistier desore enauant oeuere noetaundre dedeins la dit Fraunchise ne dehors null manere oeuere appurtenant ou spectant au mesme la Mistier sur peyne suisdicte.

La quele bille diligentment vieu et examine par les ditz Mair et Audermans pur ceo qil semble as eux les ditz deux articles estre bones ioustes et raisounables confermeront et approueront mesmes les articles en toutz leur pointz et les graunteront et ordeigneront estre desore enauant fermement et inuiolablement gardez et mys en dhue execucion pour toutz Jours.

Translation:
Be it remembered that on 5 June in the tenth year of the reign of King Henry VI after the Conquest came here before John Welles, mayor, and the aldermen in the great chamber of the guildhall of the city of London the good folk of the craft of the fletchers of the same city, and presented to the said mayor and aldermen a bill containing two articles touching the good rule and governance of their said craft, asking humbly for these to be surveyed and examined and over that they t be confirmed and approved as much for the honesty of the said craft, as for the good and profit of our lord the King and his people, the tenor of the which bill follows and is thus:

Richard Otehill and Thomas Scot, wardens, and all the good enfranchised folk of the craft of fletchers in the city of London show that whereas the servants and workers of the same craft who are hired well and lawfully to make arrows and other kinds of ammunition for the good of the King and his people and for the defence of the realm of good materials and dry wood which is delivered to them by the said supplicants, often both within the liberty of the same city and without, in their chambers and other hideouts and secret places work by night and exchange such good materials and dry wood for green wood and other false materials which cannot wear well, nor lawfully serve the King or his people, and make thereof such arrows and other kinds of ammunition, not only to the great damage and dishonour of the said supplicants, but to the grievous destruction of the King's people. May it please your good masterships to grant and ordain that the two following articles, which have been made by the common assent of

---

143 *Sic.*

the entire craft aforesaid, ordained against the said offences, be entered of record here before you in the court of our lord the King and adjudged by your wise discretions to be kept and observed for all times, for God and by way of work of charity.

Firstly, that no freeman of the same craft shall henceforth place either within the liberty of London or without any worker or servant of the said craft to work or make any arrows other than in the house where he dwells, who places or sets to work such servants, to the end and intent that due search, survey and correction can be made both of all such work, and of the material, by those who are good and qualified, to the profit of the King and his people, under the penalty of paying each time that they are convicted of doing the contrary 6*s*. 8*d*., half to the use of the abovesaid chamber of the Guildhall, and the other half to the said craft.

Item, that no man of the same craft shall henceforth work at night either within the said liberty or without in any manner of work pertaining or belonging to the same craft, under the said penalty.

Which bill, having been diligently viewed and examined by the said mayor and aldermen, because it appeared to them that the said two articles were good, just and reasonable, they confirmed and approved the same articles in every point, and granted and ordained that they should henceforth be firmly and inviolably kept and duly executed for all times.

5. Ordinances of the Fletchers' craft, providing, inter alia, *for the Company's corporate governance and journeymen's rates of pay. 11 May 1484. (LMA, City of London Letter Book L, ff. 196v-198r. A partial copy of the text is found in LMA, Journal of the Court of Common Council 9, ff. 21v-22v).*

Ordinacio de lez Fletchers etc.

Memorandum quod vndecimo die Maij anno regni Regis Ricardi tercij post Conquestum primo Gardiani et alij probi homines artis de Fletchers Ciuitatis London' venerunt hic in Curia dicti Domini Regis in Camera Guyhalde Ciuitatis predicte coram Roberto Billesdon, Maiore, et Aldermannis eiusdem Ciuitatis et porrexerunt eisdem Maiori et Aldermannis quandam billam siue supplicacionem cuius tenor sequitur in hec verba:[144]

To the right honourable Lord the Mair and the Aldremen of the Citee of London.

_____

144 LMA, Journal 9, f. 21v starts here.

Mekely besechen your goode Lordship and Maistershippes the Wardeyns and oþere goode folke enfraunchesed of þe Crafte of Fletchers of the said Citee that it myght pleas the same your goode Lordship and Maistershippes for the honour and wirship of this Citee and wele of the said Craft, and in eschewyng aswell of suche inconuenientes as often tymes happen and fall within the said Feolaship of the said Craft, as of suche deceites as myght be vsed in the same Craft to the grete hurt of the Kinges liege people and rebuke and disclaundre of the said Feolaship of the same Craft, for lak of goode rules and ordenaunces therefore to be ordeigned and made, to graunte vnto your said besechers certeyn articles hereafter folowyng by your grete auctoritces to be establisshed, enacted and had for ferme and stable from hensfurth, and here in this honourable Courte afore you to be entred of recorde for euir.

First, that all the hole Feolaship of the said Craft of Fletchers from hensfurth shall yeerly iiij tymes assemble theymself togeders at somme honest place to theym thought conuenient, than and there to commen togeders for the wele and politique guydyng of the said Craft at the iiij daies hereafter folowyng, that is to sey, in the day of the Conuersion of Seint Poule, Seint George is day, Seint Marie Magdeleyn is day and Seint Edwardes day, Kyng and Confessour, the which iiij daies shall hereafter be taken, had and kept amonges the said Feolaship as their iiij quarter daies, like as diuerse oþere Craftes of the said Citee vsen to haue and kepe. And what persone of the said Craft that commeth not to thassemble of the same Feolaship at euerich of the said iiij quarter daies withoute a reasonable excuse shall lese and pay at euery tyme that he so doeth a lb. of wex, or elles vjd. þerefore, that one half þereof to be applied to thuse of the Chambre of the said Citee, and that oþere half þereof to thuse of the said Feolaship.

Also that all suche persones of the said Craft as shalbe habled by the hole Feolaship of the same Craft to be of the lyuerey or clothing of the same Feolaship shall mowe hereafter ones in euery iij year ayenst the fest of Easter to be clothed in one lyuerey and sute by the Wardeyns for the tyme being and oþere ij honest men of the said Craft to be ordeigned and purueyed, euerich of the foresaid persones habled as is aforesaid taking a patron of the said lyuerey and to bye his clothing accordyng to the colour of the same patron. And if any of the said persones habled as is afore rehersed denye or refuse to take or were the said lyuerey or will not bye his said lyuerey accordyng to his patron, that than the same persone shall lese and pay at euery tyme that he so doeth withoute he oþerwise aggre with the saide Wardeyns and Feolaship xiijs. iiijd., to be levied, deuided and applied in manere and fourme aforesaid.

Also that the Wardeyns of the said Craft for the tyme being shall hereafter as longe as thei shall stonde in their office haue the rule and gouuernance of the

Feolaship of the said Craft, and what persone of the same Craft that hereafter will be so misavised to revile or rebuke any of the Wardeyns of the said Craft for the tyme being or any oþere man of the same Craft with vnfittyng or vnmanerly wordes or langage in oppen audience of people or in any oþere place, shall lese and pay as often as he so misbehaueth hym self in this behalf iijs. iiijd., to be devided and applied in manere and fourme abouesaid.

[f. 197r]
Also that from hensfurth no persone enfraunchesed of the said Craft of Fletchers shall werk any maner of werk belonging to the said Craft in the day of the Decollacion of Seint John Baptist, but that it be kept by the hole Feolaship of the said Craft as an holyday, shittyng in their shoppes as thei do in a double Fest, into the laude, honour and wirship of God and Seint John Baptist, vppon payn to pay vjs. viijd. as often as any suche persone dothe the contrary hereof, to be deuided in maner and fourme aforesaid.

Also that the hole Feolaship of the said Craft shall from hensfurth yeerly for euermore assemble theym self togeders at the Frere Austeyns of London vppon the said day of the Decollacion of Seint John Baptiste at an hour by the Wardeyns of the said Craft for the tyme being þereto assigned, and abide the Masse than and there before the same Feolaship to be saide. And ouer this, that the said Feolaship shall fynde for euermore a light of v tapers of wex at the said Frere Austeyns in the wirship of God and Seint John Baptiste, euery persone of the said Craft paying at euery quarter day ijd. towardes the sustentacion of the same light. And what persone of the same Feolaship that commeth not, or offereth not, at the forsaid masse withoute a reasonable excuse, or paieth not at euery quarter day as is afore said ijd. towardes the sustentacion of the said light, shall lese and pay at euery tyme that he so doth j lb. of wex or vjd. þerefore, to be deuided in manere and fourme as is afore rehersed.

Also that no persone of the said Craft from hensfurth shall neither oppen his shop, nor make shewe of any maner thing perteynyng to the same Craft vppon any Sondaies vppon payn to pay iijs. iiijd. as often as any suche persone doth the contrary hereof, to be levied and applied in manere and fourme abouesaid.

Also that euery persone of the said Craft from hensfurth shall come vnto all maner due somonse made vnto theym by the Wardeyns of the said Craft for the tyme being, or by their deputie or seruaunte in their names, atte suche tyme and place as to the same Wardeyns shall be thought conuenient. And what persone of the said Craft that absenteth hym, or will not comme at suche sommonce as is aforesaid made vnto hym withoute a reasonable excuse, shall lese and pay as often as he so dothe j lb. of wex or vjd. þerefore, to be deuided in manere and fourme aforesaid.

Also that if hereafter any persone of the said Craft fele hym self aggreued with any oþere persone of the same Craft, that than the same persone that so feleth hym self greued shall first compleyn hym and shewe his cause of greef to the Wardeyns of the said Craft for the tyme being or euer he make his compleynt any ferther, to thentent that the saide Wardeyns, the said matier of greef by theym vnderstonded, may endeuour theym to sette the parties in vnite, rest and peas. And what persone of the said Craft that doth the contrary hereof shall lese and pay at euery tyme that he so doth xiijs. iiijd., to be deuided in manere and fourme abouesaid.

Also that no maner persone of the said Craft, the which hath any app[r] entice that hath serued out the termes of his apprentishode, from hensfurth take vppon hym to make his said apprentice freman of this Citee, but that he within iiij daies after that brynge the same apprentice afore the Wardeyns of the said Craft for the tyme beyng and afore theym be sworn well and truely to hold, obserue and kepe all the goode rules and ordenaunces of the same Craft approued here by this Courte and in þe same Court entred of record. And what persone of the said Craft that doth the contrary hereof shall lese and pay as often as he so doth vjs. viijd., to be devided and applied in manere and fourme aforesaid.

[f. 197v]
Also that the Wardeyns of the saide Craft of Fletchers for the tyme being may haue full power and auctoritee at all tymes hereafter for to serche and ouersee aswell brode arrowes and boltes, as all oþere maner of artelery belongyng to the said Craft, aswell suche as shalbe brought by foreyns and other straungiers into this Citee or libertie thereof to be sold, as suche as shalbe sold by fremen of the said Craft within the same Citee, and all suche maner of artelerye as the same Wardeyns shall fynde vnlawfull or not made of seasonable stuf, thei to forfet and brynge to the Chambre of this Citee and there correction þereof to be doon, any acte or ordenaunce to the contrary of any parte of this presente acte aforetyme made in any wise not withstandyng.

Also that no persone of the said Craft from hensfurth take vppon hym to sette awerk, receive into his seruice, or hire any foreyn or oþere maner persone not being apprentice nor allowes to wirke in the same Craft withoute the same foreyn or oþere persone be first shewed vnto the Wardeyns of the same Craft for the tyme being, by theym to be examyned and vnderstonded what his connyng is. And after that the same Wardeyns can conceive what his connyng is, by their discrecions to be demed what he can deserve and is worthy to take by the yeere. And what persone of the said Craft that dothe the contrary hereof shall reu in the payne of xiijs. iiijd. as often as he so dothe, to be deuided in manere and fourme as is afore[re]hersed.

Also that all suche persones as ben admitted allowes within the said Craft shall haue and take from hensfurth for their labour for the werkmanship and makyng of thise thinges vnderwriten after the rate ensuyng, that is to sey for the makyng of c beryng shaftes of seasonable tymber, well and clenly made, with cros nokked, skynned and sered, xiiijd.; for making of c of the best beryng shaftes, well and clenly cros nokked after the best maner, and skynned and sered, as is aforesaid, xvjd.; for the makyng of c merke arrowe shaftes, well and clenly made after the fourme aforesaid, xxd.; and for the makyng of c of boltes, well and clenly made after the best forme, and after the maner abouerehersed, [-].

Also that no maner persone of the said Craft from hensfurth sette, nor do to be sette, more of any manere of artelery vppon any stall, wyndowe stok or stulp, than ij sheef, vppon the payn to lese and pay as often tymes as any suche persone dothe the contrary hereof vjs. viijd., to be applied and deuided in manere and fourme aforesaid.

Also that if hereafter it can be duely proved that any persone servyng within the said Craft be a piker or an Imbesiller of any maner thing belongyng to the same Craft to the valour of viijd., that than vppon suche proef made, the same persone to be put oute of the said Craft and neuer after that to serue within the same Craft, but if he fynde conuenient suertie to be of goode beryng and true guydyng. And what persone of the said Craft that afterward taketh vppon hym to sette any suche persone awerk contrary to this ordenaunce shall reu in the payn of xiijs. iiijd. as often as he soo dothe, to be deuided and applied in manere and fourme afore rehersed.

Also that no maner persone of the said Craft from hensfurth induce, entice or procure any mans seruaunte or apprentice of the same Craft oute of the seruice of his maister that he dwelleth with without thaggrement, consent and wille of the same his maister, vppon payne to lese and pay xiijs. iiijd. at euery tyme that any suche persone dothe the contrarye hereof, to be devided in the maner and fourme abouesaid

[f. 198r]
Also that no maner persone of the said Craft from hensfurth bere or carye to any faire, merket or any other place nerrer vnto the Citee of London than xxx myle at lest, any maner chaffer belongyng to the same Craft to sell, and that all suche chaffer as shall be caried or borne by any persone of the same Craft to any faire, merket or other place xxx myle from London or more, or it goo out of this Citee be ouerseen and serched by the Wardeyns of the said Craft for the tyme being, that it be made of goode and seasonable stuf and hable for the Kinges people to occupie. And what persone of the said Craft that dothe the contrarye of any poynte of this article shall lese and

pay as ofte as he so dothe vjs. viijd., to be deuided and applied in manere and fourme aforesaid.

Also that no maner persone of the said Craft from hensfurth haue any vnfittyng or disclaunderous langage which shuld sounde to the preiudice or hurt of þe Feolaship of the said Craft, of or vppon the making, auctorisyng or establisshyng of thise actes and ordenaunces aforewriten, or of any oþere actes and ordenaunces of the same Craft afore this approued by this honourable [Court], and in the same Court entred of recorde, or of any article or parte of theym, vppon payne of xxs. as often as any persone of the said Craft so dothe, to be deuided in manere and fourme aforesaid.

Qua quidem billa siue supplicacione lecta ac per dictos Maiorem et Aldremannos plenius intellecta quia videtur eisdem Maiori et Aldremannis quod articuli in dicta billa siue supplicacione contenti sunt boni et honesti ac racioni conson' vnanimi assensu et voluntate ordinauerunt et decreuerunt quod articuli predicti hic intrentur de recordo modo et forma quibus petuntur futuris temporibus firmiter obseruandum.

Translation:

Ordinance of the Fletchers etc.

Be it remembered that on 11 May in the first year of the reign of King Richard III after the Conquest the wardens and other good men of the craft of Fletchers of the city of London came here into the court of the Lord King in the Chamber of the Guildhall of the aforesaid City before Robert Billesdon, mayor, and the aldermen of the same City and presented to the same mayor and aldermen a certain bill or petition, the tenor whereof follows in these words:

To the right honourable Lord, the Mayor, and the aldermen of the City of London.

Mekely beseech your good Lordship and Masterships the Wardens and other good folk free of the Craft of Fletchers of the said City that it might please your same good Lordship and Masterships for the honour and worship of this City and the good of the said Craft and to avoid both such faults as often happen and occur within the said fellowship of the said Craft, as such deceits as might be committed within the said Craft, to the great hurt of the King's liege people and the shame and discredit of the said fellowship of the same Craft, for the lack of good rules and ordinances to be ordained and made for it, to grant to your said supplicants certain articles hereafter following, by your great authorities to be established, enacted and from henceforth to be kept as firm and established, and to be entered onto the record here in this honourable court before you for ever.

First, that the whole fellowship of the said Craft of Fletchers shall henceforth four times per year assemble together in some honest place thought convenient by them, then and there to consult together for the good and the prudent governance of the said Craft at the four days hereafter following, that is to say, on the day of the Conversion of St. Paul, St. George's day, St. Mary Magdalene's day and St. Edward's day, King and Confessor,[145] which four days shall hereafter be taken, had and kept by the said fellowship as their four quarter days, just as various other crafts of the said City are accustomed to have and keep. And any person of the said Craft who without a reasonable excuse does not come to the assembly of the same fellowship at each of the said four quarter days shall lose and pay every time that he so does a pound of wax or 6d., half thereof to be applied to the use of the Chamber of the said City, and the other half to the use of the said fellowship.

Also that all such persons of the said Craft as shall be admitted by the whole fellowship of the same Craft to be of the Livery or Clothing of the same fellowship shall hereafter once in every three years around the feast of Easter be clothed in one livery and suit to be chosen and arranged by the wardens for the time being and two other honest men of the said Craft, each of the aforesaid persons admitted as is aforesaid taking a pattern of the said livery and to buy his clothing according to the colour of the same pattern. And if any of the said persons admitted as is afore rehearsed shall refuse to take or wear the said livery, or will not buy his said livery according to his pattern, then the same person shall lose and pay every time that he so does without having agreed otherwise with the said wardens and fellowship, 13s. 4d. to be levied, divided and applied as aforesaid.

Also that the Wardens of the said Craft for the time being shall hereafter for as long as they shall hold their office have the rule and governance of the fellowship of the said Craft, and any person of the same Craft who will hereafter be so misadvised as to revile or rebuke any of the wardens of the said Craft for the time being or any other man of the same Craft with inappropriate or unmannerly words or language, in the open hearing of people or in any other place, shall lose and pay as often as he misbehaves in this way 3s. 4d. to be divided and applied as abovesaid.

Also that henceforth no person made free of the said Craft of Fletchers shall do any kind of work belonging to the said Craft on the day of the Decollation of St. John the Baptist, but it shall be kept by the whole

---

145 25 January, 23 April, 22 July, 13 October.

fellowship of the said Craft as a holiday, shutting up their shops as they do for a double feast, to the laud, honour and worship of God and St. John the Baptist, under pain of paying 6s. 8d. as often as any such person does the contrary hereof, to be divided as aforesaid.

Also that the whole fellowship of the said Craft shall henceforth for evermore yearly assemble at the Austin Friars of London on the said Day of the Decollation of St. John the Baptist[146] at an hour set by the Wardens of the said Craft for the time being, and attend the mass to be said then and there before the same fellowship. And over this that the said fellowship shall find for evermore a light of five tapers of wax at the said Austin Friars to the worship of God and St. John the Baptist, every person of the said Craft paying at every quarter day 2d. towards the sustenance of the same light. And any person of the same fellowship who does not come or offer at the aforesaid mass without a reasonable excuse, or does not pay at every quarter day, as is aforesaid, 2d. towards the sustenance of the said light, shall lose and pay every time that he so does one pound of wax or 6d., to be divided as is afore rehearsed.

Also that no person of the said Craft shall henceforth either open his shop, or put on display any kind of thing pertaining to the same Craft, on any Sunday, under pain of paying 3s. 4d. as often as any such person does the contrary hereof, to be levied and applied as abovesaid.

Also that every person of the said Craft shall henceforth come in response to any due summons made by the Wardens of the said Craft for the time being, or by their deputies or servants in their names, at such time and in such place as the same Wardens shall think convenient, and any person of the said Craft who absents himself or will not come in response to such a summons made as is aforesaid, without a reasonable excuse, shall lose and pay as often as he does so one pound of wax or 6d., to be divided as aforesaid.

Also that if hereafter any person of the said Craft shall feel aggrieved by any other person of the same Craft, that then the same person who so feels aggrieved shall first complain and show the cause of his grief to the Wardens of the said Craft at the time being, before he ever takes his complaint any further, to the intent that the said Wardens, having understood the said grievance, may endeavour to reconcile the parties. And any person of the said Craft who does the contrary hereof shall lose and pay every time that he so does 13s. 4d. to be divided as abovesaid.

---

146 29 August.

Also that no person of the said Craft who has any apprentice who has served out the term of his apprenticeship shall henceforth make his said apprentice a freeman of this City, unless he within four days after that brings the same apprentice before the Wardens of the said Craft at the time being, and he shall before them be sworn well and truly to hold, observe and keep all the good rules and ordinances of the same Craft approved here by this Court and in entered onto the Record in the same court. And any person of the said Craft who does the contrary hereof shall lose and pay as often as he does so 6*s*. 8*d*. to be divided and applied as aforesaid.

Also that the Wardens of the said Craft of Fletchers for the time being may have full power and authority at all times hereafter to search and oversee both broad arrows and bolts, and all other kinds of artillery belonging to the said Craft, both such as shall be brought by foreigners and other strangers into this city or its liberty to be sold, and such as shall be sold by freemen of the said Craft within the same City, and all such artillery as the same Wardens shall find faulty or not made of proper materials, shall be forfeit and brought into the Chamber of this City, and there correction thereof to be made, any act or ordinance made before this time contrary to any part of this present Act, notwithstanding.

Also that no person of the said Craft shall from henceforth set to work, receive into his service or hire any foreigner or other person not being an apprentice or journeyman to work in the same Craft without that the same foreigner or other person be first presented to the wardens of the same Craft for the time being, to be examined by them, so it may be understood what his competence is. And after the same Wardens know what his competence is, it is to be assessed by their judgment what [pay] he deserves and is worthy to take by the year. And any person of the said Craft who does the contrary hereof shall suffer in the pain of 13*s*. 4*d*. as often as he so does, to be divided as is afore rehearsed.

Also that all such persons as are admitted as journeymen within the said Craft shall henceforth have and take for their labour, for the workmanship and making of the things set out below, after the rates following, that is to say, for the making of 100 bearing shafts of suitable wood well and cleanly made, cross-nocked, skinned and dried, 14*d*.; for making of 100 of the best bearing shafts, well and cleanly cross-nocked, after the best manner, and skinned and dried, as is aforesaid, 16*d*.; for the making of 100 mark-arrow shafts, well and cleanly made in the form aforesaid, 20*d*.; and for the making of 100 bolts well and cleanly made, in the best form and in the manner rehearsed [-].

Also that no person of the said Craft shall henceforth set nor cause to be set more of any kind of artillery on any stall, window, bench or post, than two sheaves, under pain of losing and paying as often as he does the contrary hereof 6s. 8d. to be applied and divided as aforesaid.

Also that if hereafter it can be duly proven that any person serving within the said Craft be a thief or an embezzler of anything belonging to the same Craft to the value of 8d., that upon such proof being made, the same person be expelled from the said Craft and shall never after serve within the same Craft, unless he find sufficient sureties that he shall be of good bearing and true conduct and any person of the said Craft who afterwards sets any such person to work contrary to this ordinance shall suffer in the pain of 13s. 4d. as often as he does so, to be divided and applied as afore rehearsed.

Also that no person of the said Craft shall henceforth induce, entice or procure any man's servant or apprentice of the same Craft out of the service of his master with whom he dwells, without the agreement, consent and will of the same master, under pain of losing and paying 13s. 4d. every time that he does the contrary hereof, to be divided as abovesaid.

Also that no person of the said Craft shall henceforth bear or carry to any fair, market, or any other place nearer than 30 miles to the City of London any kind of merchandise belonging to the same Craft to sell, and that all such merchandise that shall be carried or borne by any person of the same Craft to any fair, market or other place 30 miles or more from London shall before it leaves this City be surveyed and searched by the Wardens of the said Craft at the time being, that it be made of good and suitable material and fit for the use of the King's people. And any person of the said Craft who does the contrary of any point of this article shall lose and pay as often as he so does 6s. 8d. to be divided and applied as aforesaid.

Also that no person of the said Craft shall henceforth have any unfitting or slanderous language which would bring discredit or hurt to the fellowship of the said Craft, about, or on account of the making, authorising or establishing of, the acts and ordinances aforewritten, or of any other acts and ordinances of the same Craft approved before this time by this honourable court, and entered onto the record in the same court, or of any article or part thereof, under pain of 20s. as often as any person of the said Craft so does, to be divided as aforesaid.

Which bill or petition having been read and fully understood by the said mayor and aldermen, because it appeared to the same mayor and aldermen that the articles contained in the said bill or petition are good and honest and reasonable, they ordained and decreed by their unanimous assent and will that the aforesaid articles be entered of record in the manner and form requested, to be firmly observed in future times.

6. Ordinance of the Fletchers' craft, prohibiting the employment of foreigners in favour of Englishmen, and the sale of unwrought fletchers' timber to such foreigners. 31 January 1503 (LMA, Journal of the Court of Common Council 10, f. 280v).

To the right honorable lord the Maire of the Citee of London and his worshipfull Brethren thaldermen of the same

In the moost humble wyse Shewen vnto your good lordship and Maistershippes youre dayly oratours the Wardens of alle the hole company Fremen of the Craft of fletchers of the Citee That where in tyme past the yongmen of the seid craft whanne they had truly served theire termes myght haue leved by theire occupacion vnto now of late that foreyns hath been sett awerke within the seid Felaship and the yong men Fremen of the same craft were Idell and not sett awerke to theire greate afterdele. Vnto suche tyme as youre seid oratours compleyned vnto the right worshipfull Syr John Shaa, knight, \thanne/ Maire by whom your seid oratours euer sythen haue been greatly releved thorough his reformacion for the continuance wherof It may please your good lordship and Maistershipes to graunt and enacte that from hensforth noon of the seid Craft of fletchers sett Any foreyns to werk within his house or within the lybertie of that Citee as long as they may haue fremen which daily bere lott and scott to serue thaime and haue ben brought vp in their seruice and fayne wold werke for theire levyng vpon payn of xl s. as often as Any of the seid craft is founden doyng contrary to this acte the oon half of the seid penaltie to goo to the Chamber of London And the other half to the vse of the seid fealiship of fletchers.

And also it may be enacted that no man of the seid fealisship of fletchers fromhensforthe sell to Any foreyn any tymber out of this Citee but if the same tymbre be redy wrought vpon payn of xl s. as often as Any of the seid fealisship shalbe found doing contrary to this acte the seid penaltie to be devyded and applied In maner and fourme afforseid this at the reueraunce of god and in the wey of charyte.
Qua quidem billa et cetera.

Translation:
To the right honourable lord, the mayor of the city of London and his worshipful brethren, the aldermen of the same:

In the most humble manner show unto your good lordship and masterships your daily supplicants, the wardens of the company of freemen of the craft of Fletchers of the City that whereas in times past the young men of the said craft, when they had truly served their terms, could have lived by their occupation, until now of late foreigners have been set to work within the said fellowship and the young men, freemen of the same craft, were idle and not set to work, to their great disadvantage, until the time when your said supplicants complained to the right worshipful Sir John Shaa, knight, then mayor, by whom your said supplicants have ever since been greatly relieved through his remedy, for the continuation of which it may please your good lordship and masterships to grant and enact that from henceforth no member of the said craft of Fletchers shall set any foreigners to work within his house or within the liberty of that City, when they may have freemen who daily bear lot and scot to serve them and have been brought up in their service, and would gladly work for their living, under penalty of 40s. as often as anyone of the said craft is found doing contrary to this act, one half of the said penalty to go to the Chamber of London, and the other half to the use of the said fellowship of Fletchers.

And also it may be enacted that no man of the said fellowship of Fletchers shall from henceforth sell to any foreigner any timber out of this City, except if the same timber be ready wrought, under penalty of 40s. as often as anyone of the said fellowship shall be found doing contrary to this act, the said penalty to be divided and applied in the manner and form aforesaid. This in reverence of God and in the way of charity.
Which bill etc.

7. Petition of the wardens and assistants of the Fletchers' Company of London to the mayor and aldermen of London to assent to a company ordinance regulating the number of apprentices taken by individual members. 6 March 1572. (LMA, Repertory of the Court of Aldermen 17, ff. 284v-285)

The wardens of Fletchers bill

Item this day the wardens and assistance of the Arte and Craft of the fletchers of London exhibyted a supplicacion or bill to this court, þe tenur wherof ensueth:

Most humbly besechen your Honor and Worshippes youre pore orators the wardens and assistentes of þe Arte or craft of the Fletchers of London þat it may please your Honor and Worshippes by your aucthoritie to confirme a certen order and constitucion by them lately agreed vpon for reformacion of certen abuses in their companie touchinge the takinge of apprentices according to the tenor hereafter ensuing. For as much as the free men of þe sayd Arte or crafte of the Fletchers of London euerye one of them at their free will and pleasure doo accustomabli take and bynde vnto them apprentice, some one apprentice, some of them tow[147] apprentices and some more and some lesse without any order to the great hinderans of þe same Arte or craft of Fletchers which now of late yeres is fallen into greate

---
147 *Sic.*

Ruyne and decaye For that Archerie is not vsed and exercised as in tymes past accordinge vnto the lawes of this Realme so þat the daly takinge and encresinge of apprentices is to be restrayned for reformacion wherof be it ordeyned and established þt euerie free man of

f. 285
of [148] þe said craft or Arte that is nowe warden and euerie one which hathe bene warden of the same arte or crafte shall or may take or reteyne and kepe in his or their service two apprentices and no more And euerie other person beinge free of þe sayd Arte or crafte beinge an householder shall and maye take reteine and kepe in his or their service one onlye apprentice and no more. And it is also agreed that yf any person of þe said art or craft offende contrarie to this order then he to paie for the same offence xx s., thone halfe therof to goe vnto the common profet and comoditye of the free men of the sayd Arte or crafte of Fletchers and thother halfe therof to þe vse of þe chamber of the cytye of London which peticion beinge redd and dilligently examined by this court þe same was Ratyfied confirmed and allowed of and ordered that the freemen beinge Fletchers with in this cytye and liberties therof shuld not take prentices other wise then In þe said bill is specified.

Translation:
Item this day the wardens and assistants of the art and craft of the Fletchers of London submitted a supplication or bill to this court, the tenor of which is as follows:

Most humbly beseech your Honour and Worships your poor supplicants the wardens and assistants of the art or craft of the Fletchers of London that it may please your Honour and Worships by your authority to confirm a certain order and constitution by them lately agreed upon, for reformation of certain abuses in their company, concerning the taking of apprentices according to the tenor hereafter following. For as much as the freemen of the said art or craft of the Fletchers of London each at their free will and pleasure customarily take and bind to themselves apprentices, some one apprentice, some of them two apprentices, and some more, and some fewer, without any order to the great hinderance of the same art or craft of Fletchers, which now of late years has fallen into great ruin and decay, because archery is not used and exercised as in times past according to the laws of this realm, so that the daily taking and increasing of the number of apprentices is to be restrained. For reformation whereof be it ordained and established that every freeman of the said craft or art that is now warden or has been a warden of the same art or craft shall or may take or retain and

---

148 *Sic.*

keep in his or their service two apprentices and no more. And every other person being free of the said art or craft, being a householder, shall and may take, retain and keep in his or their service one single apprentice and no more. And it is also agreed that if any person of the said art or craft offend against this order, he shall pay for the same offence 20s., one half thereof to go to the common profit and commodity of the freemen of the said art or craft of Fletchers, and the other half thereof to the use of the Chamber of the city of London. Which petition being read and diligently examined by this court, the same was ratified, confirmed and allowed, and it was ordered that the freemen Fletchers within this city and its liberties should not take apprentices otherwise than is specified in the said bill.

8. Report to the Court of Aldermen by Cuthbert Burkell, Hugh Offeley and William Ryder, aldermen, on a petition by the Fletchers' Company concerning the threat to their trade by the increase of the number of members of the Company, combined with the decline in the practice of archery, and ordaining that new freemen of the Company shall serve as journeymen before establishing their own shops. 12 October 1592. (LMA, Repertory of the Court of Aldermen 22, ff. 439v-440v).

Reporte for Fletchers

Item this daye Mr Burkell, Mr Offeley and Mr Ryder, aldremen, to whom the consideracion of the petycion of the companye of Fletchers was by this courte comitted did make their Reporte in wryting vnto the same Courte of their doinge therein. The tenor whereof hereafter enseweth, videlicet:
To the Righte Honorable the Lorde Maior of the Cytie of London and the worshipfull the Aldermen of the same, the Reporte of vs, Cutberte Burkell, Hugge Offeley and William Ryder, Aldermen, concerning the petycion of the Companie

f. 440
of Fletchers whiche by vertue of an order made at the corte holden the twentyth daye of Julye last paste was comitted to vs to consider of and to giue oure opynions and reporte of the same to the sayde courte which is as followeth:

Maye it please your honor and worshippes yt appeareth vnto vs aswell by examynacion of the petycion vnto your honor and worshippes by the companye of Fletchers directed as alsoe by conference had with the wardens and other the moste discreete persons of the companye that the sayde companye is greatlye decayed by the reasons in the sayde petycion alledged, videlicet: the great encrease of the Companye and the little exercyse of shoating. And for remedye therein to be had they in ther sayde peticion haue humblye desyred that yt woulde please your Honor and Worshippes

to decree that euerye yonge man whiche hereafter shalbe made free of the
sayde companye and shall vse tharte or science of Fletchers shall not sett
vpp or worke for himself vntil thende of fower yeres nexte after his or theirs
making free but to serve as Jorneymen with some one of the companye
and that after thexpiracion of the sayde fower yeres he nor they shoulde
keepe none apprentyce in twoe yeres after the fower yeres expired vppon
suche penaltye and payne as by your Honor and Worshippes shoulde seme
expedient soe as the sayde yonge men shalbe retayned and sett a worke as
Jorneymen by some of the sayde Companye during the same tearme and
haue suche reasonable wages as heretofore hathe bene vsuallye given as by
the sayd petycion more plainely appeareth.

Whiche reasons and allegacions being by vs duelye and rightlye considred,
we doe certefye your Honor and Worshippes that for to represse the greate
increase of the sayde companye and for the better preservacion of the same,
we thincke yt good and meete (yf soe yt standeth with \yor/ Honor and
Worshippes \good/ liking) That yt maye by yow be enacted and established
that noe person or persons whiche hereafter shalbe made free of the same
Companye and vse the same arte or occupacion shall within twoe yeares
nexte after he shalbe admitted to his fredome, vse or occupye the same
science for himself, but shall serve withe some one of the sayde Companye
as Jorneymen, or worke to the same Companye for the space of twoe yeres
then nexte ensewinge, for suche reasonabel wages as hathe bene by the
sayde Companye to be gyven, vppon some reasonable payne, therevppon to
be lymited, vnles anye suche person shalbe therevnto lycenced by the Lorde
Maior and Corte of Aldermen for the tyme being.

f. 440v
And further we thincke yt meete, that after the twoe yeres expired which
they shall soe serve as Jorneymen or worke to the Companye that they keepe
none Apprentyce or Apprentyces for one yere then nexte ensewing. By
which meanes we doubte not but that the yonge men which shall soe serve
shall not onlye prove better workemen, but alsoe shalbe their better able
to lyve and the Companye better preserved and kepte from that necessitye
whiche otherwyse is Likely withoute some speedye remedeye shortlye to
happen vnto them.

Which reporte being reade in this Courte was verye well liked and allowed
of and therevppon ordred that the yt shalbe entred in to the Reportarye and
observed in all pointes accordinglye.

Translation:
Report for the Fletchers

On this day Mr. Burkell, Mr. Offeley and Mr. Ryder aldermen, to whom the consideration of the petition of the Company of Fletchers was committed by this court, made their report to the court in writing, the tenor whereof follows, viz.

To the Right Honourable the Lord Mayor of the City of London and the worshipful Aldermen of the same, the report of Cuthbert Burkell, Hugh Offeley and William Ryder, aldermen, concerning the petition of the Company of Fletchers which by virtue of an order made at the court held on 20 July last past was committed to us to consider and to give our opinions and report on the same to the said court, which is as follows:

May it please your Honour and Worships, it appears to us both by examination of the petition submitted to your Honour and Worships by the Company of Fletchers and by discussions had with the wardens and other most discreet persons of the Company, that the said company has much deteriorated for the reasons alleged in the said petition, viz. the great increase of the Company in size, and the lack of the exercise of archery, and for a remedy thereof they in their said petition have humbly desired that it would please your Honour and Worships to decree that every young man who hereafter shall be made free of the said company and shall use the art or science of fletchers shall not set up [his own workshop] or work for himself until the end of four years next after he or they have been made free, but to serve as journeymen with someone of the Company and that after the end of the said four years he or they should not keep any apprentices for two more years, under such penalty and punishment [in the event of contravention] as should seem expedient to your Honour and Worships, and the said young men shall be retained and put to work as journeymen by some of the said Company during the same term and have such reasonable wages as have heretofore usually been given, as appears more plainly by the said petition.

Having duly and rightly considered these reasons and allegations, we certify to your Honour and Worships that in order to restrict the great increase in size of the said Company, and for the better preservation of the same, we think it good and right (if it pleases your Honour and Worships) that it may be enacted and established by you that no person or persons who hereafter shall be made free of the same Company and use the same art or occupation shall within two years next after he shall be admitted to his freedom use or occupy the same science for himself, but shall serve with someone of the same Company as journeymen or workers to the same Company for a period of two years then next following for such reasonable wages as it has been customary for the said Company to give, under some reasonable penalty [for contravention] to be limited thereupon, unless any such person shall be licensed to do so by the Lord Mayor and Court of Aldermen of the day.

And further we think it right, that after the two years which they shall so serve as journeymen or workers to the Company have expired, they keep no apprentice or apprentices for one year then next following. By which means we doubt not that the young men who shall so serve shall not only prove better workmen, but also shall be better able to live, and the Company better preserved and kept from the need into which they are likely to fall shortly, without some speedy remedy.

Which report having been read in this Court was very well liked and approved of and thereupon it was ordered that it shall be entered into the Repertory and observed in all points.

A Note on the Sources

Like many other livery companies, the Fletchers have few company records surviving in the original before the sixteenth century. Principal among the Company's early documentation is the grant of the Fletchers' coat of arms dating from 1467. Company records only begin to survive in earnest from 1519. From this date, there are two near-complete runs of annual, or biannual, quarterage lists, from 1519 to 1545 and 1558 to 1601 respectively. These give the dates of the election of the Company's wardens, and the names of the its members, along with a record of their attendance at the Fletchers' quarterly meetings and of any fines incurred by defaulters.

For the Company's early ordinances and regulations, we have to rely on the records of the City of London. As a company by prescription, with no royal charter of its own to grant it powers to pass regulations, the Fletchers had to rely on the authority of the City's Court of Aldermen to make their ordinances binding. Consequently, the Company's wardens presented any rules they wished to lay down for approval to the mayor and aldermen, who ultimately recorded them in the city's Letter Books. The process that preceded the approval and formal enrolment, as well as occasional proceedings taken against recalcitrant fletchers before the civic authorities can sometimes be traced through the draft records of the Court of Aldermen and Court of Common Council, the repertories of the former and journals of the latter.

The principal early sources available for individual fletchers are their wills. No original fletchers' wills are known to survive, but copies of a number of such documents from the fifteenth and sixteenth centuries are preserved in the registers of the London court of husting, the commissary court of the bishops of London, the court of the archdeacons of London, and the prerogative court of the archbishops of Canterbury, where they were presented for probate.

Finally, the archives of the English Crown offer information on royal appointments, such as those of the King's Fletchers, regulations relating to overseas trade, such as export licences, and documentation of large-scale purchases of arrows for the King's armies. Here also are found the records of the royal law courts which provide some colourful stories of wrongdoing by and against London fletchers.

Bibliography

1. Manuscript sources

Guildhall Library, London

MS 5440	Worshipful Company of Brewers, Entry Book of William Porland
MS 5977	Worshipful Company of Fletchers, Quarterage Rolls
MS 21116	Worshipful Company of Fletchers, Grant of Arms

Guildhall Library, London (now at the London Metropolitan Archives)

MS 9051	Archdeacon of London, Will Registers
MS 9171	Bishop of London, Commissary Court, Will Registers

The National Archives, Kew

C 1	Early Chancery Proceedings: Petitions
CP 40	Court of Commons Pleas, Plea (*De Banco*) Rolls
E 36	Exchequer, Miscellaneous Books
E 117	Exchequer, Inventories of Church Goods
E 159	Exchequer, King's Remembrancer, Memoranda Rolls
E 372	Exchequer, Pipe Office, Pipe Rolls
KB 27	Court of King's Bench, Plea (*Coram Rege*) Rolls
LR 15	Auditors of Land Revenue, Ancient Deeds, Series EE
PROB 11	Prerogative Court of Canterbury: Will Registers
SC 8	Special Collections: Petitions

Cornwall Record Office, Redruth

AR37	Arundell manuscripts

London Metropolitan Archives[149]

CLA/007/FN/02	London Bridge, Bridgemasters' Annual Accounts and Rentals
COL/AD/01/007	City of London, Letter Book G
COL/AD/01/008	City of London, Letter Book H
COL/AD/01/009	City of London, Letter Book I
COL/AD/01/010	City of London, Letter Book K
COL/AD/01/011	City of London, Letter Book L
COL/AD/01/012	City of London, Letter Book M
COL/AD/01/013	City of London, Letter Book N
COL/AD/01/014	City of London, Letter Book O
COL/CA/01/01/001	City of London, Court of Aldermen, Repertory 1
COL/CA/01/01/002	City of London, Court of Aldermen, Repertory 2
COL/CA/01/01/003	City of London, Court of Aldermen, Repertory 3
COL/CA/01/01/005	City of London, Court of Aldermen, Repertory 5
COL/CA/01/01/008	City of London, Court of Aldermen, Repertory 8
COL/CA/01/01/011	City of London, Court of Aldermen, Repertory 11
COL/CA/01/01/019	City of London, Court of Aldermen, Repertory 17
COL/CA/01/01/024	City of London, Court of Aldermen, Repertory 22
COL/CC/01/01/009	City of London, Court of Commons Council, Journal 9
COL/CC/01/01/010	City of London, Court of Commons Council, Journal 10
COL/CC/01/01/011	City of London, Court of Commons Council, Journal 11
COL/CC/01/01/012	City of London, Court of Commons Council, Journal 12

Worcestershire Archive and Archaeology Service, Worcester

Berington MSS, 705:24/266

2. Printed sources

The Acts and Monuments of John Foxe ed. S.R. Cattley (8 vols., London, 1838–41).

The Alien Communities of London in the Fifteenth Century: The Subsidy Rolls of 1440 and 1483–4, ed. J.L. Bolton (Stamford, 1998).

Calendar of Letter-Books of the City of London: L, Edward IV–Henry VII, ed. R.R. Sharpe (London, 1912).

Calendar of the Patent Rolls (HMSO).

Calendar of Plea and Memoranda Rolls of the City of London, 1364–81, ed. A.H. Thomas (London, 1929).

Calendar of Plea and Memoranda Rolls of the City of London, 1381–1412, ed. A.H. Thomas (London, 1932).

Calendar of the Close Rolls (HMSO).

The Estate and Household Accounts of William Worsley, Dean of St. Paul's Cathedral, 1479–1496, ed. H. Kleineke and S.R. Hovland (London Record Society, 2004).

Exeter Freemen, 1266–1967, ed. M.M. Rowe and A.M. Jackson (Exeter, Devon and Cornwall Record Society extra ser. i, 1973).

---

149 In the notes, documents in LMA have been cited by their historic description, rather than their unwieldy modern call numbers.

Letters and Papers Foreign and Domestic of the reign of Henry VIII (HMSO).

London and Middlesex Chantry Certificate, 1548, ed. C.J. Kitching (London Record Society xvi, 1980).

London Bridge: Selected Accounts and Rentals, 1381–1538, ed. V. Harding and L. Wright (London Record Society xxxi, 1995).

The London Jubilee Book, 1376–1387, ed. C.M. Barron and L. Wright (London Record Society lv, 2021).

Memorials of London and London Life in the 13th, 14th and 15th Centuries, ed. H.T. Riley (London, 1868).

Parliament Rolls of Medieval England, 1295–1504, ed. C. Given-Wilson *et al.* (16 vols., Woodbridge, 2005).

The Pinners' and Wiresellers' Book, 1462–1511, ed. B. Megson (London Record Society xliv, 2009).

Records of Early English Drama: Civic London to 1558, ed. A. Lancashire (Woodbridge, 2015).

Statutes of the Realm (11 vols, London, 1810–28, repr. 1963).

3. Secondary sources

Barron, C.M., 'The "Golden Age" of Women in Medieval London', in *Women in Southern England* (Reading Medieval Studies xv, 1989), 35–58.

————, 'Ralph Holland and the London Radicals, 1438–1444', in *The Medieval Town in England, 1200–1540*, ed. R. Holt and G. Rosser (London, 1990), pp. 160–83.

————, 'Chivalry, Pageantry and Merchant Culture in Medieval London', in *Heraldry, Pageantry and Social Display in Medieval England* ed. P. Coss and M. Keen (Woodbridge, 2002), pp. 219–41.

————, *London in the Later Middle Ages* (Oxford, 2004).

Barron, C.M., and Sutton, A.F. (eds.), *Medieval London Widows, 1300–1500* (London, 1994).

Bennett, J., '"History That Stands Still": Women's Work in the European Past', *Feminist Studies*, xiv (1988), 269–83.

Bird, R., *The Turbulent London of Richard II* (London *et al.*, 1948).

Bromley, J., and Child, H., *The Armorial Bearings of the Guilds of London* (London, 1960).

Burgess, C., '"A Fond Thing Vainly Invented": An Essay on Purgatory and Pious Motive in Late Medieval England', in *Parish, Church and People: Local Studies in Lay Religion, 1350–1750*, ed. S.J. Wright (1988), pp. 56–84.

————, '"Longing to be Prayed for", Death and Commemoration in an English Parish in the Late Middle Ages', in *The Place of the Dead: Death and Remembrance in Late Medieval and Early Modern Europe*, ed. B. Gordon and P. Marshall (Cambridge, 2000), pp. 44–65.

Cater, W.A., 'The Priory of Austin Friars, London', *Journal of the British Archaeological Association*, xviii (1912), 25–44, 57–82.

Colson, J., 'Commerce, Clusters, and Community: a Re-evaluation of the Occupational Geography of London, c.1400–c.1550', *Economic History Review*, n.s., lxix (2016), 104–30.

Curry, A.E., 'The "Coronation Expedition" and Henry VI's Court in France, 1430–1432', in *The Lancastrian Court*, ed. J. Stratford (Donington, 2003), pp. 29–52.

Davies, M.P., 'Lobbying Parliament: The London Companies in the Fifteenth Century', in *Parchment and People. Parliament in the Middle Ages*, ed. L.S. Clark, *Parliamentary History*, xxiii (2004), 136–48.

———, 'Crown, City and Guild in Late Medieval London', in *London and Beyond. Essays in Honour of Derek Keene*, ed. M. Davies and J.P. Galloway (London, 2012), pp. 247–68.

———, 'Aliens, Crafts and Guilds in Late Medieval London', in *Medieval Londoners: Essays to Mark the Eightieth Birthday of Caroline M. Barron*, ed. E.A. New and C. Steer (London, 2019), pp. 119–47.

DeVries, K., 'The Use of Gunpowder Weapons in the Wars of the Roses', in *Traditions and Transformations in Late Medieval England*, ed. D. Biggs, S.D. Michalove and A.C. Reeves (Leiden, 2002), pp. 21–38.

Doig, J.. 'Propaganda and Truth: Henry V's Royal Progress in 1421', *Nottingham Mediaeval Studies*, xl (1998), 167–79.

Dyer, C., with Penn, A.C., 'Wages and Earnings in Late Medieval England: Evidence from the Enforcement of the Labour Laws', *Economic History Review*, n.s. xliii (1990), 356–76.

Gadd, I.A., '"Ornamental for Closet or House": Printed Catalogues of the Arms of the London Livery Companies, 1596–1677', *The Coat of Arms*, 3rd ser. iii (2007), 55–66.

Galloway, J.A., Keene, D., and Murphy, M., 'Fuelling the City: Production and Distribution of Firewood and Fuel in London's Region, 1290–1400', *Economic History Review*, n.s., xlix (1996). 447–72.

Gunn, S., 'Archery Practice in Early Tudor England', *Past and Present*, ccix (2010), 53–81.

Hewerdine, A., *The Yeomen of the Guard and the Early Tudors: The Formation of a Royal Bodyguard* (London, 2012).

Holder, N., *The Friaries of Medieval London from Foundation to Dissolution* (Woodbridge, 2017).

Holder, N., Samuel, M., and Betts, I., 'The Church and Cloisters of Austin Friars', *Transactions of the London and Middlesex Archaeological Society*, lxiv (2013), 143–62.

Jessop, O. 'A New Artefact Typology for the Study of Medieval Arrowheads', *Medieval Archaeology*, xl (1996), 192–205.

Keene, D., 'Metalworking in Medieval London: an Historical Survey', *Historical Metallurgy*, xxx (1996), 95–102.

Liddy, C.D., '"Sir ye be not king": Citizenship and Speech in Late Medieval and Early Modern England', *Historical Journal*, lx (2017), 571–96.

———, 'Cultures of Surveillance in Late Medieval English Towns: The Monitoring of Speech and the Fear of Revolt' in *The Routledge History Handbook of Medieval Revolt* ed. J. Firnhaber-Baker and D. Schoenaers (Abingdon, 2017), pp. 311–29.

Lindenbaum, S., 'Ceremony and Oligarchy: the London Midsummer Watch', in *City and Spectacle in Medieval Europe*, ed. B. Hanawalt and K.L. Ryerson (Minneapolis, 1994).

London Museum Medieval Catalogue (London, 1940).

Megson, B., 'The Bowyers of London 1300–1550', *The London Journal*, xviii (1993), 1–13.

Mercer, M., 'King's Armourers and the Growth of the Armourer's Craft in Early Fourteenth-Century London', in *Fourteenth Century England VIII*, ed. J.S. Hamilton (Woodbridge, 2014), pp. 1–20.

Milward, J., *46–50 St Mary Axe, London EC3A 8EL: Post-Excavation Assessment Report* (Wessex Archaeology, 2008). Available through the Archaeology Data Service (https://doi.org/10.5284/1027838).

Oxley, J.E., *The Fletchers and Longbowstringmakers of London* (London, 1968).

Prestwich, M., *War, Politics and Finance under Edward I* (London, 1972).

Rappaport, S,, *Worlds within Worlds: Structures of Life in Sixteenth-Century London* (Cambridge, 1989).

Rex, R., 'The Friars in the English Reformation', in *The Beginnings of English Protestantism* ed. P. Marshall and A. Ryrie (Cambridge, 2002).

Richardson, T., *The Tower Armoury in the Fourteenth Century* (Leeds, 2016).

Ryrie, A., *The Gospel and Henry VIII: Evangelicals in the Early English Reformation* (Cambridge, 2003).

Spencer, D., *Royal and Urban Gunpowder Weapons in Late Medieval England* (Woodbridge, 2019).

Starley, D., 'What's the Point? A Metallurgical Insight into Medieval Arrowheads', in *De Re Metallica: Uses of Metal in the Middle Ages*, ed. R. Bork with S. Montgomery, C. Neuman de Vegvar, E. Shortell and S. Walton (Aldershot, 2005), pp. 207–21.

Stevens, M.F., 'London Women, the Courts and the "Golden Age": A Quantitative Analysis of Female Litigants in the Fourteenth and Fifteenth Centuries', *The London Journal*, xxxvii (2012), 67–88.

Strype, J., *A Survey of the Cities of London and Westminster* (2 vols., London, 1720).

Sutton, A.F., 'The Silent Years of London Guild History before 1300: The Case of the Mercers', *Historical Research*, lxxi (1998), 121–41.

———, *The Mercery of London: Trade, Goods and People, 1130–1578* (Aldershot, 2005).

———, *Wives and Widows of Medieval London* (Donington, 2016).

Sutton, A.F., and Visser-Fuchs, L., *Richard III's Books* (Stroud, 1997).

Thomas, C., and Watson, B., with Bowsher, J., 'The Mendicant Houses of Medieval London: An Archaeological Review', in *The Friars in Medieval Britain*, ed. N. Rogers (Donington, Harlaxton Medieval Studies, n.s. xix, 2010), pp. 265–97.

Veale, E., 'The "Great Twelve": Mistery and Fraternity in Thirteenth-Century London', *Historical Research*, lxiv (1991), 237–63.

Webster, P., 'The Cult of St Edmund, King and Martyr, and the Medieval Kings of England', *History*, cv (2020), 636–51.

Woodward, D., 'Wage Rates and Living Standards in Pre-Industrial England', *Past and Present*, xci (1981), 28–46.

Wylie, J.H., and Waugh, W.T., *The Reign of Henry the Fifth* (3 vols., Cambridge, 1914–29).

Young, F., *Edmund: In Search of England's Lost King* (London and New York, 2018).

4. Unpublished Doctoral Theses

Barron, C.M., 'The Government of London and its Relations with the Crown 1400–1450' (Univ. of London Ph.D. thesis, 1970).

Colson, J., 'Local Communities in Fifteenth Century London: Craft, Parish and Neighbourhood' (Univ. of London Ph.D. thesis, 2011).

Holder, N., 'The Medieval Friaries of London. A topographic and archaeological history, before and after the Dissolution' (Univ. of London Ph.D. thesis, 2011).

Hovland, S.R., 'Apprenticeship in Later Medieval London (c.1300–c.1530)' (Univ. of London Ph.D. thesis, 2006).

Kirkland, B., '"Now thrive the Armourers": The Development of the Armourers' Crafts and the Forging of Fourteenth-century London' (Univ. of York D.Phil. thesis, 2015).

Wickman, D.J., 'The Religious Allegiance of London's Ruling Elite 1520–1603' (Univ. of London Ph.D. thesis, 1995).

Index